AS Level
General Studies

Science,
Maths
and Technology

John Barnes

Shaun Best

Rob Dransfield

Text © John Barnes, Shaun Best and Rob Dransfield 2003
Original illustrations © Nelson Thornes Ltd 2003

The right of John Barnes, Shaun Best and Rob Dransfield to be identified as authors of this work has been asserted by them in accordance with the Copyright, Designs and Patents Act 1988.

Published in 2003 by:
Nelson Thornes Ltd
Delta Place
27 Bath Road
CHELTENHAM
GL53 7TH
United Kingdom

03 04 05 06 07 / 10 9 8 7 6 5 4 3 2 1

A catalogue record for this book is available from the British Library

ISBN 0 7487 7121 2

Illustrations by Oxford Designers and Illustrators

Page make-up by Northern Phototypesetting Co Ltd, Bolton

Printed and bound in Italy by Canale

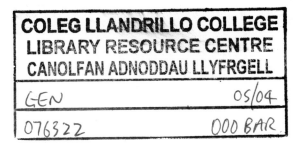

contents

acknowledgements

The authors and publishers are grateful to the following for permission to reproduce material:

- Health Protection Agency for the Tables on pp.64–65.

- *The Independent* for the extracts on pp.40–41, 114–115, 116.

Every effort has been made to contact copyright holders and we apologize if any have been overlooked. Should copyright have been unwittingly infringed in this book, the owners should contact the publishers, who will make corrections at reprint.

Photo credits:
- Associated Press (p.63, middle and bottom)
- Corbis (p.32)
- Corbis/Bettmann (p.11, top and bottom; p.35; p.38)
- Corbis/Hulton-Deutsch Collection (p.11, middle)
- Corbis/Underwood & Underwood (p.15, top)
- Digital Vision 6 (NT) (p.72)
- Digital Vision 7 (NT) (p.99)
- Genesis Picture Library (p.3, p.106)
- Granada (p.112)
- NHPA (p.39, top and bottom)
- NHPA/A P Barnes (p.52)
- NHPA/Gerard Lacz (p.134)
- NHPA/Stephen Dalton (p.15, bottom; p.59)
- Press Association (p.61)
- Rex Features Ltd/Flash press/DPPI (p.37)
- Rex Features Ltd/Rob Judges (p.116)
- University of Missouri Extension and Agricultural Information (p.63, top)
- Vodafone (p.46)
- Wellcome Trust Medical Picture Library (p.7)

1

Introduction

This book has been written to provide you with an interesting and thought-provoking outline of the science, technology and mathematical elements of the AS-level general studies specification. At the same time it takes on board the essential philosophy of general studies as a broadening and enriching experience for sixth-form students, including an investigation of contemporary themes and issues in science and technology. The text is accompanied by a range of questions and discussion points as well as examples of the required multiple-choice testing method typically used in general studies examinations.

analyse this

Which of the following areas of science interest you the most? Tick the relevant columns 1 to 5 over the page as appropriate.

1   Interests me a lot.

2   This is quite interesting.

3   I would like to know a bit more about this.

4   Not very interesting.

5   Extremely dull.

Once you have completed this exercise please turn to the end of this chapter to see a list outlining which of the above topics are included in this book. Hopefully our interests will match yours so that you can find out a little more about those things that puzzle and perplex you.

1	2	3	4	5
Genetic engineering				
Electromagnetism				
Life on other planets				
Extinction of species				
Destruction of life on earth				
Cloning				
The periodic table				
Safety of the MMR vaccine				
Evolution				
The physical properties of metals				
Chemical bonding				
The manufacture of plastics				
Sustaining the environment				
Healthy eating				

■ Which topics are the most interesting?

In the middle of July 2002, a report by the House of Commons Science and Technology Committee suggested that school science lessons are so 'boring' that they are putting many young people off of the subject for life. A report produced by the committee stated that GCSE science courses fail to reflect what students are likely to encounter in everyday life.

Students were being discouraged to think for themselves, the report said, when there were real opportunities for discussion about contemporary scientific controversies such as the measles-mumps-and-rubella (MMR) vaccine, hormone replacement therapy, asteroids, cloning and genetically modified food.

Calling for a shake-up of the curriculum, the report recommended: 'If students are to be able to see the relevance of their school science, the curriculum should include more recent scientific discoveries.'

At the same time practical work had become 'a tedious and dull activity', it continued, while course work was 'boring and pointless' and teachers and students were 'frustrated' by the lack of flexibility provided by an over-prescriptive curriculum.

Questions

1 Do the findings of the committee of MPs correspond with your own experience of learning in GCSE science?

2 Do the topics suggested by the committee of MPs correspond with your own list of interests?

3 Do you think that the way your science course was structured at GCSE would encourage more or fewer people to become scientists? Is this a

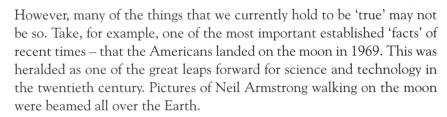

■ The nature of scientific knowledge, truth and belief

Before going on to examine some of the interesting modern-day issues in science, it is first necessary to have an idea of what science involves and what is meant by 'scientific knowledge'.

Most people would agree that we are more 'knowledgeable' than generations that lived before us. For example, we know that the Earth is not flat, and that it is not at the centre of the universe. A thousand years ago we might have met people who would argue strongly that the Earth was flat, and that their own particular village was part of the country at the heart of the universe. Over time scientists and other researchers have been able to show that these so-called 'facts' were not true.

Scientific fact or fiction?

However, many of the things that we currently hold to be 'true' may not be so. Take, for example, one of the most important established 'facts' of recent times – that the Americans landed on the moon in 1969. This was heralded as one of the great leaps forward for science and technology in the twentieth century. Pictures of Neil Armstrong walking on the moon were beamed all over the Earth.

The moon landing marked a milestone in the progress of our society. It showed that mankind was intelligent enough to create the systems to conquer space travel. However, today there are some sceptics who argue that the pictures were faked. They cite evidence to back up their case, for example:

● pictures of the earth taken from space show no stars;

● as the American astronauts planted their flag on the moon there appeared to be a breeze blowing the flag. This would be impossible on a gravity-free moon.

key
terms

science

A branch of knowledge that involves systematic observation and experiment with phenomena.

technology

The use and application of science.

knowledge

The theoretical or practical understanding of a subject.

truth

The state of being true.

belief

Holding a firm opinion.

heliocentric

Regarding the sun (rather than the Earth) as the centre of the universe.

ptolemaic system

Based on the writing of Ptolemy, a second-century Alexandrian astronomer – the theory that the Earth is a stationary centre of the universe.

Questions

1   How can we prove with certainty that the Americans landed on the moon? What does the controversy about the moon landing tell us about the nature of knowledge? What things can we be certain about?

2   Do you believe that the Americans landed astronauts on the moon in 1969? What is the basis for your belief?

analyse this

the nature of knowledge

In November 2002 a group of American scientific researchers had an article published in the journal *Science* that painted a pessimistic picture for the future.

They argued that only revolutionary advanced technology would save the Earth from relentless global warming driven by greenhouse gas emissions. They calculated that the world's primary power requirements could triple in the next 50 years, and that the temperature could climb by up to 4.5°C over the same time period.

They argued that no amount of 'regulation' by governments could solve the problem. Instead it would need dramatic leaps in technology, such as working fusion reactors, solar panels the size of Manhattan floating in space, and a 'global grid' of superconduction power transmission lines to distribute electricity without loss around the world.

Even short-term 'defensive' measures – such as removing carbon dioxide from the atmosphere and burying it in underground reservoirs, or filling the upper atmosphere with reflective molecules, or building a 1250-mile-wide mirror in space to divert some of the sun's rays, remain far beyond our capability.

In contrast, a group of Australian researchers found that our worries about the effect of greenhouse gases on the ozone layer might have been overplayed. Their measurements show that the hole in the ozone layer has started to shrink rather than to expand.

How much evidence do we need before we 'know' something?

- The American researchers believe that their predictions are based on a true assessment of the available evidence.

- The Australian researchers believe that their observations are based on a true assessment of the available evidence.

Can they both be right? Can they both be wrong? What do you think?

Scientists gather data to provide evidence to enable them to develop scientific knowledge. The American scientists had gathered and analysed a lot of scientific data to support their arguments as had the Australians. Scientific controversies occur because sets of evidence can contradict each other.

In reality it is actually very hard to develop absolute scientific truths. The nature of knowledge is that it is often tenuous. The more you investigate the nature of scientific knowledge the more likely you are to realize this. Uncertainties exist.

For example, Einstein's theory that the speed of light is a constant has recently been questioned by scientists examining light that we receive from the earliest days when the universe was created. They suggest that the speed of light may have slowed down since that time. Is what they say true or false?

The role of the scientist is to seek to improve on the 'scientific truth' that we 'know' at any one time.

Of course in the early days 'science' was a much more uncertain field of study than it is today. The early scientists had a lot to contend with:

● huge gaps in existing knowledge;

● lack of detailed published work about their field of interest;

● old-fashioned belief systems often bound up in religious ideas;

● prejudice against new ideas – often from those in authority.

■ The early days of science

In a recent book on the history of science (*Science, A History 1543–2001*, 2002), John Gribbin chose the year 1543 to mark a turning point in the development of modern day science. He chose this date because it saw the publication of two significant works:

1   Vesalius's treatise on anatomy. Vesalius used the dissection of human bodies and observation to develop a clear outline of human anatomy that corrected the errors of previous writers on this subject, including the Greeks and Romans.

2   Copernicus's *De Revolutionibus Orbium Coelestium*, which proved the superiority of the heliocentric view of the universe over the ancient Ptolemaic model that placed a stationary Earth at the universe's centre.

The publication of these two books provided an important milestone in a transition to modern science, which included:

● the development of experiments to find things out;

● the use of mathematical methods to record and interpret information;

● the development of a secular view of the world – one that was not dominated by religious explanations.

The great scientist Galileo, who developed the telescope to observe the planets, explained this new scientific approach when he wrote in a letter: 'In disputes about natural phenomena one must not begin with the authority of scriptural passages, but with sensory experience and necessary demonstrations.' In his book Gribbin shows that the development of science and technology have gone hand in hand. Science involves systematic accumulation, investigation and research into new ideas, while technology involves finding practical applications for science. Scientific investigation often involves the development of new technologies. For example, when the Americans were researching materials for their space rockets, they developed a new material with a far more down-to-earth application – the non-stick frying pan.

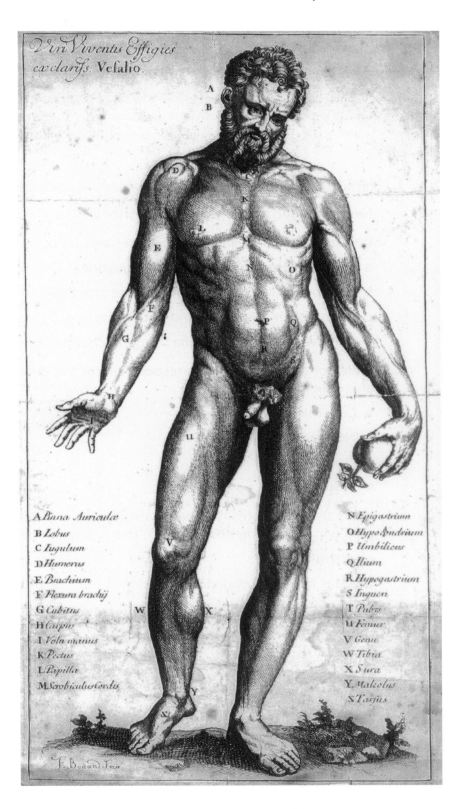

Correcting the errors of
the ancients

Gribbin also shows the importance of technology in scientific discovery.
For example, the discovery of electrons, X-rays and radioactivity – and
therefore the ensuing atomic physics of the twentieth century was given

its impetus by what seemed to be a minor piece of technological development – the development of an effective vacuum tube in the 1850s, which enabled the necessary experimental work.

In Chapter 2 we go on to examine what scientists do and then in Chapter 3 we look at the nature of the scientific method, and further develop the relationship between science, technology and progress.

Questions

Here are some multiple-choice questions.

1 Which of the following is the best description of technology:

a detailed research into scientific questions;

b the application of science to solving practical problems;

c use of experimentation and data collection;

d observation of phenomena using precise mathematical calculations?

2 Which of the following was responsible for the development of accurate anatomical investigation:

a Copernicus;

b Newton;

c Ptolemy;

d Vesalius?

3 If a researcher states that her investigations lead her to argue that the ice caps will all have melted by 2020, this is an example of:

a scientific truth;

b belief based on evidence;

c a point of view;

d an unfounded opinion.

4 Copernicus was able to show that:

a the Earth is the centre of the universe;

b the Americans did not land on the moon in 1969;

c heliocentric explanations are superior to Ptolemaic ones;

d the sun can be viewed through a telescope.

5 Which of the following is *not* a characteristic of modern scientific approaches:

a the use of mathematical tools in observation and experimentation.

b an emphasis on religious explanations for natural phenomena;

c an emphasis on experimental and observational methods;

d the development of a secular view of the world?

6 Which of the following is an example of technology rather than science:

a investigations into the properties of light;

b the development of practical uses for newly discovered materials;

c experiments with the optical properties of lenses;

d the observation of the movement of the planets?

analyse this

After reading this chapter and carrying out the activities involved in it, what are your views about the following:

1 Is there such a thing as scientific truth?

2 How would you go about developing scientific knowledge?

3 What is the value of scientific knowledge?

4 What is the relationship between science and technology?

In the next chapter we go on to examine the role of the scientist and the technologist.

■ Topics included in this book

This book deals with the following:

- genetic engineering – see Chapter 4;

- life on other planets – see Chapter 6;

- extinction of species – see Chapter 8;

- cloning – see Chapter 4;

- safety of the MMR vaccine – see Chapter 7;

- evolution – see Chapter 3;

- sustaining the environment – see Chapter 8;

- healthy eating – see Chapter 7.

2

Doing science

analyse
this

Answer the following questions:

1   What do you think is meant by using a scientific approach?

2   Can you find definite proof by carrying out scientific experiments?

3   How should the results of scientific experiments be recorded?

Marie Curie 1867–1934 discovered and isolated radium and polonium.

■ What is a scientist?

John Harman explains what a scientist is in an amusing way:

In 1883 William Whewell came up with the idea of calling scientists scientists. Before then they'd been labelled 'natural philosophers' which I think sounds rather flash. Well, they might have called themselves scientists, but we wouldn't have let them get away with it now, as they were mostly amateurs or hangers-on. A scientist (as we all know) is supposed to:

- *form a hypothesis (idea),*

- *conduct an experiment to try it out,*

- *then announce his or her theory to the waiting world.*

As it happens, most science wasn't practised by this method (and still isn't). Some scientists don't even do experiments, while others get their facts by experiments and then never even bother to produce a theory. Having said that, this was one of the most productive periods in scientific development – especially in Europe. (From John Harman's, A Suspiciously Simple History of Science and Innovation.)

Louis Pasteur 1822–95. His discovery that the fermentation of milk and alcohol was caused by micro-organisms resulted in the process of pasteurisation.

■ Scientific method

Harman goes on to explain how one of the most eminent scientists of all time, Isaac Newton, used a scientific approach:

Top of the boffin pile was a guy called Isaac Newton who escaped the plague in 1665 when he dashed out of Cambridge and went home to Mum in Woolsthorpe. The following year was to be the most creative in his life. He wrote it all down in this book called Principia *which was to be the top work on physics for over 200 years. Unlike Descartes, the first modern philosopher, he based his theories on what he saw, rather than what he thought after he'd seen it. He called it the method of analysis and synthesis, but you get the general idea. This was OK as far as it went, but it's fair to say that Newton went on to use intuition to deduce and predict things which he later proved by experiment.*

The above extract outlines two ways in which the scientist can work:

1 *Analysis and synthesis.* You make observations, for example through a telescope or by observing everyday events and patterns around you. You record data, and organize these data in a systematic way in order to identify patterns and trends. Using your analysis you are able to organize your findings into laws and general tendencies showing your understanding of how the world around you is organized. In this way you become more knowledgeable.

Albert Einstein 1870–1955. He formulated the special theory of relativity and the general theory of relativity and made major contributions to the quantum theory.

key terms

analysis

The division of a physical or abstract whole into its constituent parts to examine or determine their relationships. A statement of the result of this.

synthesis

The process of combining objects or ideas into a complex whole.

intuition

Instinctive knowledge or belief.

induction

Inference of a general law from particular instances. Using an inductive method often involves experiment and observation, the findings and results of which can be used to derive general laws.

deduction

A logical conclusion arrived at through a process of reasoning.

2 Intuition, deduction, prediction and experimentation. Using reason, you sense that particular patterns and relationships exist in the real world. You then use reason to make deductions about these relationships and patterns, enabling you to make likely predictions that X is related to Y. You then carry out experiments to provide evidence that your initial deductions are valid.

At one time it was fashionable to state that science was unique because it employed a single scientific method, which involved:

- putting forward a hypothesis;

- making predictions;

- thinking up tests to test the validity of the hypothesis.

A sceptical experimenter should then try to see if the hypothesis is falsifiable by setting up tests that would prove the hypothesis to be false.

In reality, scientists use a range of methods, often depending on what branch of science they are in. For example, astronomers may concentrate largely on observation rather than experimentation.

■ The importance of a questioning approach

One of the greatest dangers in science is that of having a pet theory and then simply seeking evidence to support it.

Karl Popper, in his book *The Logic of Scientific Discovery,* has shown scientists that they need to be more careful.

Popper was at pains to emphasize the importance of the logical fallacy of drawing general conclusions from limited evidence. In everyday life this is a common logical error that is rarely challenged. He was highly critical of sampling techniques and probability theory.

One of his major criticisms of sampling was that, in the case of many hypotheses or theories, the potential body of evidence a researcher might collect is insignificantly small in relation to the total body of evidence. The more general the theory, the larger the potential body of evidence and the less likely it is that a particular researcher will have collected a sample of evidence that is representative of the whole. Popper never tired of warning against the dangers of generalizing from limited evidence.

If a hypothesis or a theory purports to be general, as is often the case in the natural sciences, then it is critical not to seek evidence in support of the theory but evidence that contradicts it. General statements, which are held to be universally 'true', only need one counter-example, one piece of evidence that contradicts the statement, to render the statement false. No amount of favourable evidence will demonstrate that a general statement is true, but one piece of unfavourable evidence will show that it is false.

One of Popper's favourite ways of exemplifying this fact was to propose a general thesis that there are no green swans in existence. He would then wander around the room encapsulating circles of space in both arms, repeatedly proclaiming. 'There are no green swans in this space. There are no green swans in this space.' Each of these spaces he offered as evidence in support of his thesis on the absence of green swans. The absurdity of the procedure was self-evident.

■ The importance of observation

One of the most important approaches available to the scientist is that of observation, which is all about looking and then making a systematic record of what we see.

For example, Darwin was able to notice that particular types of birds had developed characteristics that enabled them to cope better with their environment. Once he had started to develop ideas about evolution he was able to start observing in a more purposeful way. There are a number of key aspects of scientific observation. These include:

- looking at familiar objects and events, but seeking to examine them with a fresh eye, rather than taking what we see for granted;

- paying attention to the detail of what we see;

- thinking about what we see, and asking further questions to help us see more clearly;

- looking purposefully trying to focus on important aspects rather than looking at everything in an unfocused way;

- using a systematic approach;

- looking at what we already know and then building on that.

The purpose of observation should be to develop high-quality information. Quantity of information can be important, but quality is more important.

analyse this

'evidence supports stopping hormone replacement treatment'

A major study in America whose results were published in July 2002 showed that women taking hormone replacement therapy (HRT) increased their risk of breast cancer, heart disease and strokes. The study was halted after it became clear that a brand similar to that taken by hundreds of thousands of British women was damaging patients' health rather than improving it.

The American trial found a 26 per cent increase in invasive breast cancer among the women taking the pills, a 41 per cent increase in stroke risk, a 22 per cent increase in heart disease, and a doubling of blood clots. Against that, there were fewer cases of colorectal cancer and hip fractures.

Calling a premature end to the trial, the doctors involved said that the particular combination of oestrogen and progestin should no longer be prescribed. 'The whole purpose of healthy women taking long-term oestrogen/progestin therapy is to preserve health and prevent disease', they wrote in the *Journal of the American Medical Association.* 'The results of this study provide strong evidence that the opposite is happening for important aspects of women's health.'

Questions

1 Do you think that hormone replacement treatment is a good thing? Why?

2 Why is it essential for scientists to monitor the effects of HRT?

3 Why have the tests been stopped in America?

4 What evidence would you need to have to decide whether similar tests should be stopped in the UK or not?

5 Why is evidence collection and observation an important aspect of scientific monitoring?

analyse this

being scientific – Rachel Carson

The following case study shows how a scientist operates, and how, by working in a methodical and systematic way, a scientist can produce the sort of evidence that can change social practice. It focuses on the work of the American scientist, Rachel Carson, who wrote the famous book *Silent Spring*.

Rachel Carson

Rachel Carson stands out as one of the most important figures of the twentieth century in radically changing our perception of the importance of nature. As a scientist she was able to point out the harm that pesticides were and are doing to the environment. She collected a mass of evidence to back up her claims. Her work shows the difference that scientists can make through the gathering of detailed research information to support their claims. She was an important voice standing out against the powers of the giant multinational corporations that dominate agri-business.

Her book *Silent Spring* was first published in 1962, and provided a scientific exposure of the effects of the indiscriminate use of chemicals by man. In *Silent Spring* she described how pesticides and insecticides were applied almost universally to farms, forests, gardens and homes with scant regard to the consequent contamination of our environment and the widespread destruction of wildlife.

A bird singing in spring

The structure and layout of Carson's *Silent Spring* gives a clear indication of the scientific approach that was used. The book (in its paperback form) is only 220 pages long, but at the end it contains 40 pages of references. As a trained scientist, Carson set out to support her findings and analysis with detailed evidence that she gained from a variety of sources. Like many ecologists, Carson's concern for the environment stemmed from an initial concern for her own immediate environment, which then spread to a wider concern for the globe. Initially she became aware of issues relating to crop spraying in her immediate vicinity, but through her contacts across the world she could see that this was a much wider problem. In the course of her work, Carson developed a network of scientists, journalists and activists across the world who helped her document environmental abuse.

Carson's research involved making phone calls, studying direct evidence and sifting through thousands of reports to build up a case against the use of poisonous chemicals.

Carson employed a young researcher, Bette Haney, to help her with her work and the method used by the two is clearly described in Linda Lear's biography of Carson:

At the beginning of each week, the two would meet and review the bibliography Carson had prepared on index cards. The evidence of what DDT and the other chemicals did to the land and to wildlife was available in the agricultural journals Carson assigned Haney to read. Bette would read the articles and write summaries of them. If an article was particularly important, Rachel starred it and asked for specific information. Carson would call the librarians and make sure the material she wanted was available before she sent Haney in to work. Sometimes Rachel wanted to read an important article or parts of it herself, in which case Bette went to the library, pulled the material and had it laid out for Rachel.

The structure of the arguments that enabled her to present the case against pesticides and insecticides involved building up overwhelming evidence by means of painstaking research into an area that first interested her in 1938 and was finally to lead to the publication of Silent Spring *in 1962. Examples of evidence she collected included reports of the contamination of cow milk from pastures sprayed by DDT and the reproductive failures of various birds after ingesting poisoned insects . . . the thrust of her arguments was that human populations were being put at risk by the use of new chemicals. One of her vivid examples was that in 1957 pesticides were used in New York to attempt to prevent 'an infestation of gypsy moths'. Carson wrote 'The gypsy moth, is a forest insect certainly not an inhabitant of cities. Nor does it live in meadows, cultivated fields, gardens or marshes. Nevertheless, the planes hired by the United States Department of Agriculture and the New York Department of Agriculture and Markets showered down the prescribed DDT – in fuel-oil – with impartiality. They sprayed truck gardens and dairy farms, fish ponds and salt marshes. They sprayed the quarter-acre lots of suburbia drenching a housewife and making a desperate effort to cover her garden before the roaring plane reached her, and showering insecticide over children at play and commuters at railway stations. At Setauket a fine quarter horse drank from a trough in a field which the planes had sprayed; 10 hours later it was dead.' Finally, she felt that she had a compelling case that showed how pesticides menaced the ecological balance and were a direct threat to human health.*

Prior to publication she was able to assert that:

As I look over my reference material, I am impressed by the fact that the evidence on this particular point outweighs by far, in sheer bulk and also significance, any other aspect of the problem. I have a comforting feeling that what I shall now be able to achieve is a synthesis of widely scattered facts, that have not heretofore been considered in relation to each other. It is now possible to build up, step by step, a really damning case against the use of these chemicals as they are now inflicted upon us.

She called her book *Silent Spring* because 'over increasingly large areas of the United States, spring now comes unheralded by the return of the birds, and the early mornings are strangely silent where once they were filled with the beauty of bird song.'

Carson's work as a scientist emphasised the continuity of human life, and the importance of preserving this continuity through our relationship with nature. If we want to move forward we have to do so in conjunction with nature.

Questions

1 How did the scientific methods that Carson used help her to build up a convincing case?

2 What does Carson's work tell us about the role of the scientist?

3 Can science present an objective case, in debates like the one outlined relating to the use of pesticides?

ecology

The study of the relationship between organisms and their environment.

■ The importance of experiments

Experiments are one of the most important approaches used by scientists. Using this method, scientists are able to gather information that gives them clearer ideas about how the world works. It is useful to test and compare different theories to see which are most useful in providing explanations of the world's behaviour.

The purpose of carrying out an experiment is to see whether an idea stands up to testing in controlled conditions.

We can use experiments to test hypotheses. For example, on turning on my computer to write this text, I might find that there is no power going to the computer terminal. Based on my previous experience I can set out a number of hypotheses to explain why this might have happened:

1 There is a power cut.

2 The switch is not turned on at the socket.

3 A fuse has gone in my fuse box.

4 There is a fault with the computer.

I can check each of these hypotheses in turn. First of all I can test hypothesis 1. All I need to do here is to check whether the light in the room is working or not. If it is I can assume that there is no power cut. For hypothesis 2 I can turn the switch on and see if this has the desired effect. If this is successful then I do not need to bother with hypothesis 3 and examine the fuses in the fuse box. Of course, I might test out each of the three hypotheses and find out that my computer is still not working requiring a fourth hypothesis.

A good hypothesis should allow you to make predictions and then test them against reality. For example, if there is a power cut then the rest of the electrical appliances in the house should not be working – and so on.

The results of testing a hypothesis should support or alternatively weaken a particular hypothesis.

analyse
this

Columbus tests his hypothesis

Hypotheses have been described as 'hunches' about how a thing that you are interested in works. The danger of such 'hunches' is that they can become hobbyhorses and 'scientists' can go to great lengths simply to try to prove that they were right all along.

It has often been pointed out that a very good example of the use of hypothesis is provided by Columbus's discovery of America, which has many features of a classic discovery in science. Columbus was obsessed with the idea that if the Earth were round he could reach the East Indies by sailing west.

You should all be familiar with the story of how Christopher Columbus set out in 1492 to discover a sea passage to the East Indies. Believing that the world was round he thought that all he needed to do was to sail west to discover the lands that he was looking for. When he reached America he believed that he had found the land that he was looking for.

Notice the following points, which are typical of many supposedly 'great breakthroughs' in thinking:

1   The idea was not a new one; however, Columbus had obtained some additional information leading him to the hypothesis.

2   He met great difficulties in getting someone to finance the voyage (in the same way that many scientists find it difficult to raise funds to explore new ideas). It was also extremely hard to test the hypothesis – in Columbus's case he was faced by atrocious weather conditions and the near mutiny of his crew.

3   He did not find the expected new route, but, instead, found a new half of the world.

4   Despite all evidence to the contrary, he clung to the belief that he had found a new route to the Orient.

5   He received little credit or reward during his lifetime.

6   Evidence has since been brought forward that he was by no means the first European to reach America.

Questions

1 Can you think of reasons why scientists might find difficulty in gaining research funds to test major hypotheses, such as hypotheses relating to the link between smoking and cancer? Can you think of other examples where it would be difficult to gain the research funds?

2 Why might pioneering scientific work be difficult to carry out?

3 Why do you think scientists often discover, through their pioneering research, findings that they had not initially imagined?

4 Why do you think that scientists and investigators often cling on to their original hypotheses and ideas?

5 Can you think of examples of major new ideas where the original scientists carrying out the research received little recognition during their lives?

W. Bolton describes the experimental method in the following way:

The stages that are involved in experimental work are:

1. Aim
The aim of the experiment needs to be defined and perfectly clear before any further work starts. What is the purpose of the experiment? What is to be found out? For example, the aim of an electrical experiment might be to find out whether a particular resistor obeys Ohm's law. Another experiment might be to find a value for the thermal conductivity of some material. Another experiment might be to investigate the chemical reaction between iodine and aqueous alcohol and determine the factors affecting the rate of the reaction.

2. Plan
When the aim is clear, the experiment needs to be planned. This means making decisions about such matters as what measurements are to be made, how the measurements are to be made and what instruments are needed. Thus with an experiment to find out whether a resistor obeys Ohm's law the measurements to be made are current and voltage. What size currents and voltage are likely to be involved and so what meters should be selected?

3. Preparations
Once the experiment is planned, preparations must be made to carry out the experiment. This involves collecting and assembling the required instruments and making certain you know how to operate them. For example, if the

experiment requires the use of an instrument with a vernier, do you know how to read such a scale? In carrying out the experiment, are there any health and safety factors which need to be taken into account? For example, will you need a fume cupboard or perhaps may care need to be exercised because of high voltages?

4. Preliminary experiment

In some cases a preliminary experiment might be needed to find out whether the method you propose or the instruments you have selected are suitable. For example, with the use of meters such as ammeters and voltmeters, a preliminary experiment might be used to determine whether the current and voltage ranges of the instruments are adequate to enable the full range of measurements to be made.

5. Doing the experiment and making measurements

The next stage is to carry out the experiment, making such measurements as are required. Steps should be taken to minimise errors by eliminating systematic errors (a systematic error is one that is constant through a set of readings) e.g. adjusting an ammeter so that it reads zero when there is no current, and techniques adopted to reduce the impact of random errors, e.g. taking a series of measurements and using the mean values. All measurements and details of the instruments used should be recorded. For example, in the measurement of a temperature the instrument used needs to be recorded because it could have an impact on the data obtained. A mercury-in-glass thermometer, because it is relatively slow reacting, is likely to lag behind a fast-changing temperature change and so affect the results obtained, whereas a thermocouple is much faster reacting. Thus the temperature readings indicated by these could differ.

6. Repeating measurements

Often there can be a need to repeat some measurements in order to verify that the first set of results obtained can be reproduced and can thus be relied on. It is often worthwhile doing at least some preliminary analysis of the data before putting all the equipment away in order to check whether there is some oddity about a particular measurement or set of measurements and repetition is necessary. For example, with a multi-range ammeter you might have misread the range for some readings.

7. Analysis of the data

Analyse the data to find out what the data tells you, taking into account the accuracy of measurements, and estimate the accuracy of the final result.

8. Report

Finally there needs to be a report of the experiment in which the findings are communicated to others.

analyse
this
an alternative view of scientific method

Read through the following extract and then answer the questions that follow.

Finagle's laws ... or why nothing in Research and Development happens the way it should.

First law
If anything can go wrong with an experiment, it will.

Second law
No matter what result is anticipated, there is always someone willing to fake it.

Third law
No matter what the result, there is always someone eager to misinterpret it.

Fourth law
No matter what occurs, there is always someone who believes it happened according to his pet theory.

The law of the too solid goof.
In any collection of data, the figure that is most obviously correct – beyond all need of checking – is the mistake.

Corollary I
No one who you ask for help will see it either.

Corollary II
Everyone who stops by with unsought advice will see it immediately.

Advice to Experimenters

i.   Experiments must be reproducible – they should all fail in the same way.

ii.   First draw your curves – then plot the readings.

iii.   Experience is directly proportional to equipment ruined.

iv.   A record of data is useful – it indicates you've been working.

v.   To study a subject best, understand it thoroughly before you start.

vi.   In case of doubt make it sound convincing.

vii.   Do not believe in miracles – rely on them.

viii. Always leave room to add an explanation when it doesn't work.

A mathematical notation of Finagle's work has also been developed. Here, however, there seems to be some confusion, because two other names enter the picture: 'fudge' and 'diddle' factors are also used to considerable advantage by scientists and engineers.

However, John W Campbell feels there is a different basic structure behind the Finagle, fudge, and diddle factors. The Finagle factor, he claims, is characterised by changing the Universe to fit an equation. The fudge factor, on the other hand, changes the equation to fit the Universe. And finally, the diddle factor changes things so that the equation and the Universe appear to fit, without making any real change in either.

For example, the planet Uranus was introduced to the Universe when Newtonian laws couldn't be made to match known planetary motions. This is a beautiful example of the application of the Finagle factor.

Einstein's work leading to relativity was strongly influenced by the observed facts about the orbit of Mercury. Obviously a fudge factor was introduced.

The photographer's use of a 'soft-focus' lens when taking portraits of women over 35 is an example of the diddle factor. By blurring the results, photographs are made to appear to match the facts in a far more satisfactory manner.

To our knowledge, this is the first clear enunciation of the scientific method. All our vast sum of human knowledge has been derived with these as the basic tools. By having them in writing for the first time, perhaps our children can build even better futures than the best we envision today.

(Source: *IRE Student Quarterly,* September 1958)

Questions

1 In what way does the above present a view that science is not always 'scientific'?

2 Explain two ways in which findings might be adjusted to support a pet hypothesis or theory.

3 How does the article suggest that the results of scientific enquiry can be 'adjusted' to prove what is required.

4 Give an example of fudges and diddles with which you are familiar, or have used yourself to win an argument.

■ Writing up scientific reports

Scientific reports are typically set out in the following fashion:

● *Summary* – an outline of the findings of a scientific experiment or investigation.

● *Aim* – sets out the purpose of the scientific investigation or experiment. Usually just a brief statement.

● *Hypothesis* – an explanation of the hypothesis that was investigated.

- *Method* – an explanation of the methods employed to carry out the research.

- *Results/findings* – what was found out; tables of results, graphs, descriptions of findings.

- *Conclusion* – brief concluding section.

Setting out reports in this way enables clear communication between scientists so that they are able to replicate experiments and to check results.

Questions

1 A hypothesis is:

a a statement of established facts;

b an outline of results that have been verified;

c a suggested explanation for a group of facts;

d a scientific explanation of a group of phenomena.

2 The deductive method involves:

a observing phenomena and reporting the results;

b experimenting in the laboratory;

c arriving at conclusions through a process of reasoning;

d setting out general laws based on a process of observation.

3 Karl Popper criticised sampling because he felt that it:

a was too time consuming to collect a detailed sample;

b only draws on a small part of total available evidence;

c is representative of the available evidence;

d is difficult to choose an appropriate sampling method.

4 Popper believed that an appropriate approach to general theories is to:

a seek further evidence that supports the general theory;

b seek evidence that contradicts the general theory;

c carry out experiments to support the general theory;

d carry out observations to support claims made by the theory.

5 In developing a scientific case against the use of pesticides and insecticides, Rachel Carson:

a sought to build up a wealth of supporting evidence to identify a causal link;

b sought to provide a few colourful illustrations to back up her case;

c built up evidence from a narrow selection of evidence sources;

d focused exclusively on experimental work to prove causal links.

6 A good hypothesis:

a reveals scientific truths about relationships between scientific phenomena;

b cannot be tested using experimental methods of investigation;

c should allow the user to make predictions and then test them against reality;

d is nothing more than a 'hunch'.

7 Which of the following provides an appropriate order for stages in experimental work (note that only some of the stages are included):

a analyse the data, then set out your aim, and then produce your results;

b produce a report, then outline your plan, and then carry out a preliminary experiment;

c plan your experiment, then take measurements, and then produce a report;

d analyse your data, then set out your aim, and then make measurements?

8 Which of the following techniques could be used to reduce the impact of random errors in experimental work:

a taking a series of measurements and using mean values;

b giving equal importance to all measured values;

c only recording every other measurement in a series;

d only carrying out an experiment one time?

9 Which of the following are most likely to be found in the results/finding section of a scientific report:

a the aim of the investigation;

b an explanation of the hypothesis to be investigated;

c an explanation of the methods used;

d tables and charts showing recorded information?

10 Who was the author of *Silent Spring*:

a Isaac Newton;

b Isaac Asimov;

c Rachel Carson;

d Albert Einstein?

11 Is there such a thing as a 'scientific approach'? If there is what does it entail?

12 What is the purpose of carrying out scientific experiments?

13 What is the role of observation in science? What is special about scientific observation?

14 How should the results of scientific experiments be recorded?

3

The nature of scientific objectivity and the question of progress

Questions

1 Does science make us more knowledgeable?

2 Can science help us to unlock the secrets of the universe? Give evidence to support your claims.

3 Do you believe in a theory of 'everything'?

4 Are scientists the right people to develop theories of everything?

In the previous chapter we examined key aspects of scientific method and showed how scientists gather evidence to support their theories and ideas as well as seeking evidence that might contradict them. We now move on to further examine the nature of scientific objectivity.

■ Objective and subjective approaches

There is an essential difference between objective and subjective approaches and statements. An objective statement is a statement of

key term

objective

This means that observation is undistorted by emotion or personal bias. Objectivity occurs where an object or event exists independently of perceptions of an individual's conceptions.

what is – for example, this book is written in black ink on white pages. You can prove whether or not this is the case simply by using your eyes, although many other objective statements will need more rigorous testing. Objective facts are real ones that exist, uncoloured by our feelings or opinions. In contrast, subjective statements and facts are ones that are influenced by our personal preferences and views – for example, my view that Manchester United is a better football team than Arsenal. Of course, I can make objective statements about the teams such as 'Manchester United beat Newcastle United on 23 November 2002, while on the same day Arsenal lost 3–2 to Southampton'.

Scientists set out to be objective wherever possible. Being objective involves seeking to examine the world around us in an unbiased way – treating it as an external object outside ourselves that has an existence and character of its own. Any number of objective scientists should be able to conduct experiments and observe phenomena that produce the same results and observations. This would not be the case if scientists operated in a 'subjective way', putting their own thoughts and feelings into interpreting the data that they observe. The objective scientist therefore seeks to carry out fair tests that can be replicated and to set out results and make predictions in an objective way. This is much easier to do in sciences that are concerned with the study of inanimate objects such as astronomy, and geology. It is much more difficult when studying human beings because scientists are much more likely to be subjective – in these cases it is much more difficult to take the human out of the scientist.

■ The nature of belief, knowledge and truth

In the introductory chapter we asked the question 'How much evidence do we need to know that something is true?' It is helpful to explore this question in a lot more depth.

Scientific reasoning is primarily concerned with setting out statements about the nature of the world around us and relationships within that world.

True statements set out the way that things might or might not be, whereas false statements are ones that are not true. In other words, true scientific statements correspond with reality.

Scientific statement	→ Corresponds with ←	Reality
	→ True ←	

Belief

We use the term belief to refer to a situation in which an individual is of the opinion that a statement (in this case a scientific statement) corresponds with reality. Of course, the belief may be unfounded – for example the belief that the world will come to an end in 2010 may or may not be unfounded as the event may or may not happen.

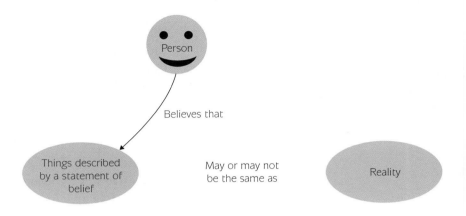

Knowledge

The scientific method that we described in the previous chapter can be seen as the way in which we acquire scientific knowledge. This raises the question of what we mean by 'knowledge'. Clearly, a first step in developing knowledge is belief – for example to know that the Earth revolves around the sun we must first believe that this is the real situation. However, there is more to knowing than simply believing.

A major step forward from belief to knowledge is that of having justifications – good reasons for holding our beliefs. Scientists must therefore provide justifications and evidence if they are going to make claims to scientific knowledge, such as making and recording observations of the relationship between the earth and the sun.

Truth

A further step in knowing rather than just believing is that a statement needs to be true.

A true statement is one where:

1 A person believes that the statement is true.

2 The person is justified in believing that the statement is true.

3 The statement is in fact true.

Of course, as we suggested in the previous chapter, the nature of knowledge is that it is, in fact, frequently uncertain. Knowledge should be seen as being provisional – the truth often eludes us.

However, the scientist will seek to find truth.

■ The creation of 'good theories'

From ancient times to the nineteenth century the term 'science' tended to be used to refer to the organization of a body of theories in a logical fashion aimed at acquiring or revealing some aspect of knowledge.

Science was associated with 'good explanations' and 'good theories' based on criteria such as being 'in accord with revealed truth', or 'testable by experience'.

In the nineteenth century what counted as science was set out in more detailed form in terms of the 'logical positivist' way of looking at things, which provided a number of criteria for judging scientific explanations, namely:

- claims to knowledge of the world are justified only by experience;

- the test of a theory is the success of its predictions;

- judgements of value have no place in science. In other words science involves finding out and stating *what is* rather than *what ought to be*.

key terms

empirical

Derived from experience or evidence rather than by theory.

The logical positivists believed that knowledge would *progress* over time because scientists would continually create new theories which they would test out in the light of experience. 'Unscientific theories would be rejected, while theories and laws which prove to be true will be accumulated.'

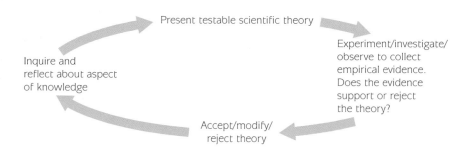

Present testable scientific theory

Experiment/investigate/observe to collect empirical evidence. Does the evidence support or reject the theory?

Accept/modify/reject theory

Inquire and reflect about aspect of knowledge

Karl Popper and the idea of falsification

Karl Popper (*The Logic of Scientific Discovery*, 1959) argued that scientists can spend their time more productively seeking out information that contradicts a theory as well as seeking to build up evidence to support it. He used the example of the statement that 'there are no green swans!' However, if a green swan could be found this would immediately contradict the theory that there are no green swans. Scientists frequently get bogged down with finding lots of evidence to back up their own theory. The reality is that the best way of supporting a theory is to seek ways of contradicting it. To Popper, therefore, seeking 'falsification' is a better approach than seeking 'verification'.

Popper was committed to the scientific approach of seeking evidence to support theories, but he made one major modification. This is that we should be concerned as much with the process of scientific discovery and theory creation as with the structure and status of the statements that we claim to be scientific.

■ Science, technology and progress

Very few people would disagree with the statement that science and technology have contributed to the progress of mankind. Today, we do not have to rub together two bits of wood to create fire or spend hours hunting and fishing to provide a subsistence meal, and we can travel for our holidays to exotic locations and enjoy the use of a range of sophisticated consumer goods such as computers, washing machines and cars.

Scientific research involves investigating the universe around us and finding applications for scientific discoveries. Most countries of the world have active scientific communities made up of individual men and women who can share their ideas through published journals, conferences, and internet communication.

Technologists play an important role. Typically they work in the following way (all the stages are interconnected):

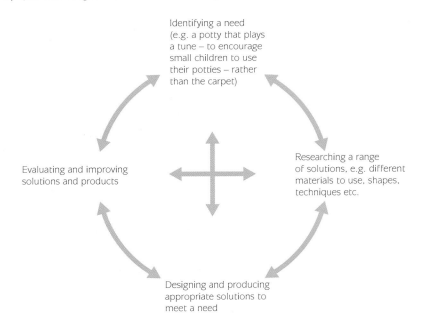

Identifying a need (e.g. a potty that plays a tune – to encourage small children to use their potties – rather than the carpet)

Researching a range of solutions, e.g. different materials to use, shapes, techniques etc.

Designing and producing appropriate solutions to meet a need

Evaluating and improving solutions and products

Technologists are able to use the findings of science, for example about the properties of materials, new ways of creating polymers and fibres, and so forth, and to apply these discoveries to creating products that meet people's needs.

Technologists therefore provide a bridge between scientific discovery and human progress through the development of goods and services that make us better off. For example:

- technologists develop new housing and building materials;

- food technologists develop exciting new types of foods;

- communications technologists develop new ways of communicating with other people, for example through the internet, as well as advanced forms of transport such as high-speed trains.

Technologists are able to produce a range of products and systems enabling progress to take place. A *product* might be a new pot, a new fuel-efficient car and so forth. A *system* could be a traffic flow system, or a way of processing orders in a warehouse or supermarket.

Of course, we need to ask serious questions about what 'progress' means. For example, today many households benefit from owning a motor car, but the pollution that it creates causes asthma, and if there are too many cars on the roads this leads to society incurring costs such as wasted time and money, and irritation.

The great leap forward

Magnus Pyke, in his book *The Science Century*, argues that the combination of science and technology in the nineteenth century enabled the great leap forward in manufacturing. The outline of his argument is that:

> *The main change brought about by science and the technology derived from it has been due to the injection of scientific thinking into the actual organisation of industry itself . . .*

> *Scientific knowledge advances when people doubt what they are told and design experiments or tests to see whether it is true. And if they find that what they previously thought to be a fact is not exactly so, or that an accepted explanation from a group of facts does not fit the truth of the matter, then it is up to the scientist to make more accurate observations of the fact or to conceive out of his inner consciousness a better explanation to co-ordinate what he has observed of Nature.*

> *Not long ago, the doctrine upon which industry was based was one entirely remote from the challenging philosophy of science. The principle of there being a master with his apprentices, or a guild or society of tradesmen into which newcomers could only enter after serving an apprenticeship is the very opposite of science. An apprentice serves his master for a number of years*

31

during which time he learns the ancient art or mystery of weaving or baking or printing or whatever the operation may be. In due time, he in his turn teaches a younger man what he learned. The process allows a bootmaker, let us say, to make an excellent pair of boots but it does nothing to progress the art of bootmaking which, when the old bootmaker retires or dies, is in exactly the same state as it was when he learned the trade as a boy . . .

In the nineteenth century, as the scientific atmosphere gradually began to pervade more and more aspects of life, things began to change. The idea that to make a particular article – a pair of boots, a copper kettle or a piece of cloth – was a craft that had to be laboriously acquired in a period of training extending over years was gradually replaced by what the economists of the day called 'the division of labour'. Instead of one seamstress making a shirt, a number of women, each now equipped with a sewing machine, made a part of the shirt – and another woman assembled the various portions into the final finished garment. This process of operation quickly extended to almost every kind of manufacture . . .

The significance of the division of labour which justified the respect paid to it by nineteenth-century manufacturers was that it represented the beginnings of the application of scientific thinking to the organisation of industry and not merely to the processes used. This meant that manufacture was no longer based on the laboriously learned methods of the past but on experimentally established procedures which were liable to further immediate change should they be found on trial to be capable of improvement.

The final development of this phase of science-stimulated factory management was introduced by Henry Ford in 1914.

One of Henry Ford's production lines – the application of scientific thinking to industry

At first, Ford merely arranged for a small belt to carry the magnetos along a table at which sat a number of operators, each of whom had one simple thing to do. A man – or woman – might even be engaged all day long in slipping a

washer over the projecting end of a screw; the next man sitting beside him would then put a nut on to the screw, his entire time being spent in putting nut after nut on to screw after screw; then another man would screw the nut on. In due time, however, Ford began to think out the nature of the motor-car making process as a whole as if it were a scientific problem. And soon he conceived the idea that the moving assembly line could be applied also to the assembly of the car chassis and that then a further assembly line could just as effectively be set up to assemble the body and another to assemble the now completed body with the completed chassis. Whereas before this original idea was introduced it had taken 12 hours and 35 minutes of work to put a Ford car chassis together, seven months after the moving assembly belt process had been introduced a completed chassis came off the belt every 84 minutes.

Ford and his mass-produced motor-car represent the crest of the wave of the First Industrial Revolution. In the last part of this eventful century of applied science from, say, 1920 to 1960, there came a second wave: the Second Industrial Revolution. The sign of its arrival was Carothers' production of nylon. Henceforward there was to be deliberate use of scientific thinking directed to the solution of set questions. Individual firms set up research laboratories to make useful discoveries, and, indeed, useful discoveries were made. Not many of these were of first-rate originality but each of them contributed its mite or added efficiency or convenience or novelty and hence justified the expense involved by a steady increase in profit. For industry as a whole, the progress year by year was rapid. Each new model of motor-car was faster, safer, more convenient to drive and, in real terms, cheaper than the last. Glass windscreens – to take one example – became first shatter-proof, then clear and transparent, then curved as well. Chemical discoveries led to the development of detergents better than soap and, of course, to plastics and synthetic textile fibres of increasing beauty, utility, durability, and strength.

Finally, the development of electronic devices made it possible to build general purpose digital computers which enabled mental operations to be done automatically and mass produced, just as Ford's travelling belt, served by a series of men using power tools – each one designed only for a single restricted operation – had brought mechanical mass production into operation.

Science, technology and progress

The impact of science takes place at three levels.

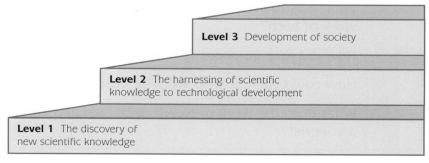

Level 3 Development of society

Level 2 The harnessing of scientific knowledge to technological development

Level 1 The discovery of new scientific knowledge

The impact of science

For example, the scientist Michael Faraday carried out studies into electro-magnetism, which he published in the 1880s. These studies were then developed into the practical technology of the dynamo, which was further developed for the use of electric street lighting. Today, electric power is used in most parts of the globe and is used to improve living standards – we can cook with electricity, work our computers using electric power, read books into the night, and enjoy leisure activities such as the cinema and discotheques where the source of power is electricity.

The cumulative effect of millions of scientific and technological developments is the progress of society, for example:

- through new cures for heart disease and other diseases;
- through the development of new modes of communication;
- the development of more varied leisure activities;
- the increased productivity of food industries coupled with greater variety of diet, and so forth.

■ The great scientists – how did they work?

If progress as we know it is based on the foundation of work carried out by scientists and technologists, we need to know a little bit more about how scientists work and the major contributions that they have made.

The following section therefore examines the work of three famous scientists:

- Isaac Newton;
- Charles Darwin;
- Albert Einstein.

Questions

Read through the passages on each of these scientists then answer the following questions:

1 What scientific approaches did each of the individuals in the section use to find scientific truths?

2 What was the relationship between theory and empirical evidence in the work of each?

3 How did they go about finding out proof?

4 How could each of their work be described as scientific?

5 What does the work of Newton, Darwin and Einstein tell us about being a scientist?

Isaac Newton (1642–1727)

Sir Isaac Newton, the scientist who was able to read the hand of nature

Isaac Newton is regarded by many to be the most important Englishman and scientist of all time. Albert Einstein said of Newton:

Nature was to him an open book, whose letters he could read without effort. The conceptions which he used to reduce the material of experience to order seemed to flow spontaneously from experience itself, from the beautiful experiments that he ranged in order like playthings and describes with an affectionate wealth of detail. In one person he combines the experimenter, the theorist, the mechanic, and not least, the artist in exposition. He stands before us strong, certain, and alone; his joy in creation and his minute precision are evident in every word and figure.

What distinguished Newton from mere mortals was his ability to focus on a problem until he had solved it. Whereas ordinary people may be able to concentrate on a problem for a few hours, Newton was able to maintain his concentration until he had come up with an explanation. He trained his intellect from an early age and liked to work in seclusion with his books, papers, telescope and scientific equipment. He was extremely impatient and hated disturbance.

The significance of Newton's work extended beyond the areas that he investigated and experimented in. More importantly it gave rise to what is referred to as Newtonian science, the belief that through detailed experiments, investigation and rational thought we are able to find out how things work, to unlock the secrets of nature. In the seventeenth century Newton and the other great scientist, Galileo, set the trend by arguing that the truth could be gained through reasoning and the scientific method, and this was to replace superstition and tradition.

Newton used two main methods to solve the riddles of science. One method was to work out things in his head using a deductive approach. The other was that of observation, experimentation, recording results and coming to conclusions.

There is the story of how he informed Halley (of comet fame) of one of his most fundamental discoveries of planetary motion. 'Yes,' replied Halley, 'but how do you know that? Have you proved it?' Newton was taken aback 'Why, I've known it for years,' he replied. 'If you'll give me a few days, I'll certainly find you a proof of it' – as in due course he did.

Newton was a master of the scientific method. His experiments were always set out in immaculate detail and the results recorded in a clear and systematic way. The Newtonian method has been at the heart of scientific approaches to the present day with its emphasis on combining intellect with experiment to find results that help us to know more about things that puzzle us.

Newton first studied at Trinity College Cambridge, and then later taught there. It was during his time at Cambridge that he became such an eminent scientist. He became totally wrapped up in the study of the universe, and in nature and its secrets, carrying out his famous experiments on light, gravity and other forces. His rooms at Cambridge were surrounded by a small garden, and he had a telescope mounted at the top of his stairs. When he was working on a problem he would hide himself away for weeks on end.

The law of gravity

The most famous idea associated with Isaac Newton is that of the law of gravity. The story is that one day, while Newton was sitting under an apple tree, an apple fell on his head, which led him to speculate about how gravity affects everything on Earth. It is possible that this story has some truth in it because as a scientist Newton used observation and evidence to create his theories.

In 1666 he developed a theory of universal gravitation that explained the movement of the moon around the Earth. His work was based on the observation of the moon's motion.

Much later (1687) Newton devised another theory that anticipated space travel. He argued that if a cannon could be fired with sufficient force, the cannonball would speed off in a straight line into space.

Experiments on light

Newton's experiments and his publication of his work *Opticks* proved to be one of the most influential breakthroughs in scientific method. The work was as significant for what it taught other scientists about how to go about their work as it was in documenting the discoveries about light.

Between 1665 and 1666 Isaac Newton carried out experiments in a darkened room. He put a glass prism in a beam of sunlight streaming through a small hole in the wall, and saw it split into the colours of the rainbow: red, orange, yellow, green, blue, indigo and violent. When he placed a second prism in the coloured beam, he saw the light rays bend back and become white again.

The development of a reflecting telescope

Isaac Newton built the first reflecting telescope. It had concave mirrors instead of lenses. It was only 15 cm long but had a magnification of 40 times.

Laws of motion

Newton set out a number of laws of motion that provide the basis for much of modern thinking on this subject.

In his first law of motion (1687) he stated that every object remains in motion, or stays motionless, unless acted on by another force.

His second law of motion showed that the force required to slow down an object with less mass is smaller than one required to slow one with more mass, which helps to explain why it is easier in rugby to stop normal-sized players than it is to stop Jonah Lomu. This law provided a major breakthrough in providing a precise concept of force.

Over the years many English rugby players have been able to experience Newton's second law of motion at first hand – in trying to stop Jonah Lomu

The third law of motion was that for every action there is an equal and opposite reaction. So, for example, in a jet engine the force pushing back behind the engine leads to an equal and opposite force propelling the engine forwards.

Mathematical and other breakthroughs

In the field of mathematics Newton's major achievements were his discovery of the binomial theorem, and of mathematical calculus.

In the field of dynamics Newton provided a solution to the problem of Kepler motion when, through his experiments, he was able to show that a gravitating sphere attracts at points outside it as if all its mass were concentrated at the centre. He also provided a solution to the problem of colliding bodies in the law of centrifugal force.

Conclusion

Newtonian science dominated approaches to science until the present time. Newton provided a model of how to conduct experiments and how to go about finding scientific proofs. There is some evidence that Newton, in preparing his most famous work, *Principia Mathematica,* was held up almost to the last moment by lack of proof that you could treat a solid sphere as though all its mass was concentrated at the centre, and only found the proof a year before publication. However, his genius was in continually chasing the solution to scientific puzzles by concentrated thought and experiment.

Questions

1 Do you think that scientists like Newton are able 'to read the stories behind nature and to discover many of the mysteries of the universe'?

2 Do you think that scientists like Newton are able to discover truth?

Charles Darwin developed the theory of evolution

Charles Robert Darwin (1809–82)

Most people have some awareness of the importance of Charles Darwin. He was the scientist who uncovered the story of human evolution over time, and revealed the way in which species come to adapt to a changing environment.

Darwin's work helps us to understand the answers to questions that are of importance us all, such as how we have evolved from basic creatures like apes into sophisticated human beings able to develop complex technologies, and to groom ourselves (in many cases) into sophisticated individuals capable of intricate thought and communication patterns.

Darwin gathered evidence about animal and plant species from a range of different geographical locations, which he painstakingly recorded. He was then able to use this empirical evidence to draw out connections enabling him to build a theory of evolution.

While studying at Cambridge, Darwin was fortunate enough to be asked to sail on HMS *Beagle* as the ship's naturalist.

The ship went on to make an epic voyage, which today would provide an ideal 'gap-year' adventure for any student, sailing to Cape Verde, South America, the Galapagos Islands, Tahiti, New Zealand, Australia, Mauritius, and South Africa. The voyage lasted from December 1831 until October 1836 and today reads like a list of expensive and exotic holiday locations.

The origin of species by descent with modification

Darwin developed the theory of natural selection, which is widely known as 'the survival of the fittest'. In simple terms this means that those species and members of a species that are most suited to their environments are most likely to survive, while less-suited individuals and species will perish. The theory of the origin of species by descent with modification was based on four lines of observation by Darwin.

1 Observations made in South America and the Galapagos Islands. Here Darwin was able to observe the replacement of species in neighbouring areas by different but related species.

2 Collection of fossils and recording of the details of related living species in the same continent showing similarities of types over time.

3 Observing similarities between the birds on the Galapagos Archipelago and in neighbouring South America.

4 The observation of differences, related to their manner of life, between species of birds on different islands. It appeared that birds developed clear differences according to the environment in which they lived.

Observations and the resulting evidence therefore provided Darwin with enough support to indicate that species are modified during descent, in order to adapt to their environments.

By 1838 Darwin was convinced that individuals better adapted to their environment would leave more offspring and therefore gradually change the type of species in the direction of more effective adaptation to the environment. For example, on an island on which hard nuts grew, requiring birds to crack them open with their beaks, those birds with the sharpest beaks would be most likely to survive. Thus the genes of sharp-beaked birds within a species would be passed on to a new generation, whereas those with less sharp beaks would perish – 'the survival of the fittest'. On the Galapagos Islands, Darwin identified 13 species of finch. He examined them carefully and realized that they must all have been descended from one species from the South American mainland. The original finch ate seeds and lived on the ground. However, in the course of time its offspring had evolved different shaped beaks and patterns of life. For example, seed-eating finches have big and powerful beaks whereas insect-eating ones have thinner pointed beaks.

A seed-eating finch (Bullfinch)

Darwin was aware that in the battle for survival different species compete for food. Those most successful at using the food supplies available to them are the most likely to succeed and flourish. For example, in this country the red squirrel was to be found almost everywhere when the countryside was covered in woods and forests. However, with the arrival of the grey squirrel from the USA and the disappearance of many wooded areas to be replaced by open fields, the red squirrel has retreated into mountainous areas such as the Highlands of Scotland.

An insect-eating finch (Warbler)

Darwin kept detailed records of all that he observed in his *Journal of the Voyage of the Beagle,* and in 1859 his work, *The Origin of Species*, was published. Darwin was an avid recorder of evolutionary trends in plants as well as animal species.

Conclusion

Darwin's work was of groundbreaking importance because it gives us a much better understanding of our own development, as well as of the development of other species. Not only does it give us a picture of our own place in the long march of history, but it also provides an interesting base for genetic research into the nature of selective breeding and the modification of species – for example in the genetic modification of rice so as to make it more disease and climate resistant.

analyse
this

The following extract is from the *Independent* dated 16 July 2002. Study it and answer the questions that follow.

Two of Britain's best-loved native trees are engaged in a Darwinian struggle for survival as they adapt to warmer temperatures brought by climate change.

The ash and the oak are racing one another to be the first species to sprout leaves and thereby take the biggest share of the summer sunlight.

Research suggests that, so far, the oak is the runaway winner in a competition that heralds an overhaul of the biological make-up of Britain's woodlands.

The oak's success has rendered obsolete an old Lincolnshire saying that generations of amateur meteorologists have used to predict summer rainfall.

The adage – 'If the oak is before the ash, then we're in for a soak' – bears testimony to the traditionally equal struggle to leaf first between the species.

But global warming has now tipped the balance in favour of the oak, according to a new study by the UK Phenology Network, a collaboration between the conservation charity, the Woodland Trust and the Centre for Ecology and Hydrology in Cambridgeshire.

Thousands of volunteers have been monitoring climate change by recording the time of the first flowering of plants, the first sightings of birds and the first leaves appearing on trees.

Nick Collinson, a conservation policy adviser for the Woodland Trust said that observations showed that oak was now leafing 10 days earlier than it did 20 years ago. Ash leafed before oak 30 per cent of the time over the last 160 years but in the last 30 years it has leafed first less than 10 per cent of the time.

Oak is moving ahead of ash because oaks react well to temperature change whereas ash is thought to depend more on light to trigger its leaf growing mechanisms.

Experts at the trust believe the temperature change has set off a classic Darwinian 'survival of the fittest' competition in Britain's native forests.

'The old rhyme probably had some truth in it at one time but it may have little significance soon because if temperatures keep rising it is unlikely that ash will ever leaf before oak,' Mr Collinson said.

More than 400 plant-eating insects depend on oak, compared to only 68 for ash, and oak supports the widest variety of species of all native British trees.

But Mr Collinson said declining numbers of ash trees would alter a long established balance in British woodland with unpredictable results.

'If we see important native species that have been part of our ecosystem for thousands of years outcompeted by another species we need to know more about it.'

Ash is still flourishing in open countryside, but in woodland areas the early arrival of leaves on oak trees means it is deprived of light, hampering its growth and ability to support insects, mosses and lichens, which may be forced to move north to find suitable habitats.

Dr Tim Sparks, of the Centre for Ecology and Hydrology, said the future for many woodland species was bleak. 'Urgent research is needed into issues such as competitive advantage and life cycles,' he said. 'We need to know what the knock on effects will be for our unique communities of plants and animals.'

More than 17,000 people are contributing to the phenology project, the largest scheme of its kind in the world and the Woodland Trust needs more people to observe natural events in woods, gardens and parks. Recording forms are available from www.phenology.org.uk.

Questions

1 What appears to have triggered the 'classic Darwinian struggle for survival' outlined in the extract?

2 According to the evidence provided in the article, which species is most likely to win the struggle?

3 What would be the likely outcome of such a result?

4 How might human intervention change the result of this struggle?

Albert Einstein (1879–1955)

Einstein is one of the most celebrated scientists of the twentieth century, and we often refer to someone who is highly intelligent as a 'real Einstein'. Einstein was able to apply mathematical principles to the study of physics.

The theory of relativity

Einstein took as his basic principle the fact that the velocity of light in empty space is constant and the same throughout the universe, however we are moving and however a source emitting light is moving relative to us.

Einstein was able to develop from this a mathematical system that made the laws of physics the same for observers on bodies that were moving relative to each other with a fixed velocity.

Einstein called this the 'special' theory of relativity, which he outlined in a paper in 1905. Einstein continued to work on developing and improving this theory and began to consider the question of relativity and gravitation.

In 1915 he published his 'general' theory of relativity, which was concerned not only with observers who were moving with a fixed velocity, but also those moving with a changing velocity – observers who are accelerating with respect to each other. As gravity causes bodies to accelerate in their motions towards one another, this meant that the force of gravity could be brought into the theory.

Einstein's work thus built on earlier work of Newton – for example showing that light is attracted by gravitation, and helping to explain the strange rotation of the planet Mercury.

One of the most important conclusions of Einstein's relativity theory is the relation of the mass of a body to its energy. The formula is often quoted as:

$$E = mc^2$$

Where E is the energy, m the body's mass, and c the velocity of light.

This formula provides a means for expressing the energy of a body in terms of its mass, and so shows that we can consider mass as a form of energy.

It can be seen that mass can be converted into energy. If we destroy mass we can produce energy, as happens deep within the sun and in other stars, and also provides the basis for the production of the atom and hydrogen bombs.

Nuclear energy used in power generation is obtained from the gradual release of 'relativity' energy by the destruction of matter.

Questions

1 To what extent can the work of scientists like Einstein be used to enable the progress of mankind?

2 To what extent can the work of scientists like Einstein be used to retard progress?

■ The importance of design and technology

Scientists help us to understand how things work, but it is technologists who take this work forward in designing and developing applications that help us. Everything that you use at home, at school or college has its origins in one simple, perhaps ingenious, idea. However, it takes more than creative thinking to make a good idea work. It takes someone, somewhere, to turn that idea into a realistic and affordable solution that people want.

Technology offers the potential to make life easier and more enjoyable; each new technology providing increasing benefits.

Donald A. Norman, in his book *The Design of Everyday Things*, says that there are at least 20 000 everyday things we use that are the result of modern technology:

> *Start by looking about you. There are light fixtures, bulbs, and sockets; wall plates and screws, clocks, watches and watchbands. There are writing devices (I count twelve in front of me, each different in function, color, or style). There are clothes, with different functions, openings and flaps. Notice the variety of materials and pieces. Notice the variety of fasteners – buttons, zippers, snaps, laces. Look at all the furniture and food utensils; all those details, each servicing some function for manufacturability, usage, or appearance. Consider the work area: paper clips, scissors, pads of paper, magazines, books, bookmarks. In the room I'm working in, I counted more than a hundred specialised objects before I tired. Each is simple, but each requires it own method of operation, each has to be learned, each does its own specialised task, and each has to be designed separately.*

Norman advocates user-centred design and suggests that products should be made so that they are usable and understandable. He states: 'make sure that (1) the user can figure out what to do and (2) the user can tell what is going on.' He goes on to say:

> *The operation of any device – whether it be a can opener, a power generating plant, or a computer system – is learned more readily, and the problems are tracked down more accurately and easily, if the user has a good conceptual model. This requires that the principles of operation be observable, that all actions be consistent with the conceptual model, and that the visible parts of the device reflect the current state of the device in a way that is consistent with that model. The designer must develop a conceptual model that is appropriate for the user, that captures the important parts of the operation of the device, and that is understandable by the user.*

Standardization and technology

All of us use thousands of everyday things. When we think about it, it is remarkable that we are so knowledgeable and skilful. For example, we can:

- use a knife and fork;
- operate the cooker;
- use electrical appliances;

- cut the grass using a lawnmower;

- use the washing machine, and so forth.

We can use what are often complex pieces of machinery because they have been simplified by designers for us, and also because they have been standardized. Donald Norman writes that:

> *If we examine the history of advances in all technological fields, we see that some improvements naturally come through technology, others come through standardisation. The early history of the automobile is a good example. The first cars were very difficult to operate. They required strength and skill beyond the abilities of many. Some problems were solved through automation: the choke, the spark advance, and the starter engine.*

> *Arbitrary aspects of cars and driving had to be standardised:*
> - *Which side of the road people drove on*
> - *Which side of the car the driver sat on.*
> - *Where the essential components were: steering wheel, brake, clutch pedal, and accelerator (in some early cars it was on a hand lever).*

> *Standardisation is simply another aspect of cultural constraints. With standardisation, once you have learned to drive one car, you feel justifiably confident that you can drive any car, any place in the world.*

Norman is critical of current computers because he believes that there is not enough standardization, which causes difficulties for users. He states that:

> *when we have standardisation of our keyboard layouts, our input and output formats, our operating systems, our text editors and word processors, and the basic means of operating any program, then suddenly we will have a major breakthrough in usability.*

■ Recent developments in communications technology and transport systems

Developments in communications technology, transport and other new systems lie at the heart of our modern lifestyles.

We use the term globalization to describe a world in which the barriers of time and distance have shrunk – and in which we are able to travel to the other side of the world in less than a day and to communicate by phone and internet link often in seconds rather than minutes. It is through revolutions in technology that these distances have shrunk.

Examples of developments in communication technology

While previous generations benefited from breakthroughs in communications such as the invention of the telephone and the wireless, the present generation has been the prime beneficiaries of the communications revolution, which goes from strength to strength.

Examples of developments in communications include:

- the rapid development of computer technology and the growth of the internet;

- mobile phone developments;

- the revolution in transport systems.

The rapid development of computer technology and the growth of the internet

Moore's law states that computer power doubles every 18 months. The price of computer power has already fallen 10 000-fold within a single generation. Growth of 35 per cent in computer power dwarfs the 5 per cent per year power growth delivered by steam engines and their successor, electric engines, between 1869 and 1939. At the same time the expansion of computer use has been extraordinary. Use of the internet is growing literally exponentially. It took radio 37 years to reach a global audience of 50 million. Television took 15 years. Yet it took the World Wide Web just three years after the development of the web browser in 1994.

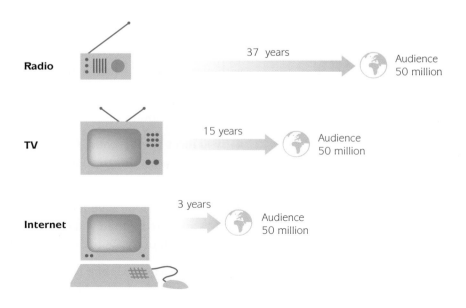

It seems likely that, in this new century, the impact of the ICT revolution will hit us with more and more force as its influence begins to strike home. The economic historian, Paul David, showed how it took US industry 40 years to reorganize to exploit the electric dynamo efficiently. Once it made full use of this new technology, the impact was staggering, leading to mass production and mass consumption.

It seems likely that ICT will have the same sort of impact in transforming production systems on a worldwide scale.

The internet was born in 1969, the year of the Apollo moon landings. For a number of years it was used mainly by computer buffs or 'netties' who wallowed in their own brand of computer jargon but, today, it has become widely accessible to a broader group of users and, every day, more people are joining the internet. Today there are over 50 million people connected to the internet, although use tends to be dominated by white, male, upper-income groups in the world's richest countries.

The internet began life as a defence network that linked the computers of a few thousand researchers and military personnel. Today the internet might carry almost anything – the late-night ramblings of a Star Trek fan, the plight of a Third World refugee, and computer games software. No matter how obscure the information, it will probably exist on the internet.

Mobile phone developments

Most young people carry a mobile phone around with them and mobile phones are becoming more complex. The new generation of mobile phones is typified by Vodafone Live! This is a completely new world of mobile services, for the first time bringing together the power of colour, sound and pictures for richer communication. Vodafone Live! brings together an initial range of services including picture messaging, colour 2D/3D gaming, realistic ring tones, alerts and information in colour and with pictures, all of which can be accessed from a picture menu.

The sort of services available on this new generation of phone enable the user to do the following:

● you meet an old school friend on the street, have a drink in a coffee bar and you want to share this moment with you friends – you can take a picture with a built-in camera and send it immediately;

● you are on a long train journey, you have read all your magazines and you are bored – then you can download a Vodafone Live! game such as Pacman or Space Invaders.

Of course, because mobile telephony is a rapidly developing art, by the time this book goes into publication there will be an increasing number of services offered to phone users.

The revolution in transport systems

Transport systems, whether they be on land, sea or air, or even space travel, have all experienced dramatic and ongoing revolutions. On land, the motor car has come to dominate the design of cities with huge spaces being allocated for the movement and parking of cars. As early as 1961, the manager of the Department of Traffic in Los Angeles reported that one-third of the area of the city was required for transportation facilities.

We are increasingly seeking alternative forms of transportation in cities – transport that does not clog and congest in the same ways. This is leading to the return of tramway systems and integrated public transport schemes with out-of-town car parking.

The volume of air traffic continues to grow year by year, as more passengers are able to afford to pay ever-falling air prices. This leads to increasing congestion in the air, and increasing worries about air traffic control systems.

Complex technical systems have been designed to better manage modern transport flows as is illustrated by the following case study.

analyse this

SCOOT systems

In this country the SCOOT (split cycle and offset optimization technique) is widely used by local authorities to manage the movement of traffic in their area.

In urban areas traffic signals are close together, and they need to be co-ordinated to create the most efficient movement of traffic. It is easy to organize sets of lights so that they are at green when a driver is following a set route, but this is not so easy to manage when drivers are choosing different routes, as is frequently the case in an urban area – some may be going to the shops, while others want to go in the other direction to the gym, while a third group may want to cut across to go to a football match.

The SCOOT system is based on computer simulations. Sensors are set up near junctions and crossings in a particular area providing the input to the system. These sensors provide computers with up-to-the-minute information about traffic flow. The computer receives this information along fibre optic links. The computer then analyses the data, and can then amend the traffic signal timings and the 'offset' between signals – the phasing between one traffic signal and the next along a section of road.

The SCOOT system maximizes the efficiency of traffic movement in the following ways:

- Optimizing the split. The amount of time given to 'green' (the 'green split') is varied by the SCOOT system according to the intensity of traffic movement.

- Optimizing the cycle. The amount of time in a particular cycle – red, amber, green can be altered. When there is a low flow of traffic, for example five o'clock in the morning, there can be a very quick cycle so that traffic is not held up. However, at busy times, for example when children are going to school at 8.30 a.m., then there may need to be a longer cycle.

- Optimizing the 'offset'. It is important to link the various parts of the system together – the lights that comprise the overall system within the urban area. If this is well managed drivers will be able to flow from one green light to the next.

Traffic flow provides us with a good example of how technology aids us to live better lives. A well-organized system makes everyone happier and saves money and time.

The components of the system are:

- inputs – information about actual traffic flow;

- processes – the co-ordination of lights, management of the offset, and so on;

- outputs – traffic signals enabling smooth traffic flow.

The role of the technologist is to provide the systems, for example the computer and lighting technology, and to organize the systems and processes that enable it all to work smoothly giving us a much higher standard of living – what we refer to as progress.

Questions

1 Which of the following is an objective statement?

a Manchester United will win the Premier League for the next 10 years.

b The Manchester United home strip is red and white.

c Manchester United is always more stylish than Arsenal.

d Everyone loves David Beckham and the England team.

2 If there were a statement that everyone in the world believed to be true:

a it would have to be true;

b it would have to be false;

c it could either be true or false;

d it would be false until proven to be true.

3 A scientific statement:

a is one based on value judgements;

b is true if it corresponds with reality;

c is one that does not add to knowledge;

d is merely a hunch.

4 Which of the following is incorrect in relation to true statements?

a The statement is in fact true.

b Scientists believe that the statement is true.

c Scientists are justified in believing that the statement is true.

d The statement is based on subjective interpretations of events.

5 Karl Popper argued that scientists can spend time most productively by:

a building evidence to justify their opinions;

b seeking cases that refute their ideas;

c repeating experiments that back up their ideas;

d rejecting other people's theories in favour of their own.

6 Which of the following is most likely to be the work of a technologist?

a Applying scientific discoveries to product development.

b Laboratory experiment.

c The deduction of scientific theories.

d Pure research into the properties of chemical elements.

7 Which of the following was responsible for the development of science-stimulated factory management:

a Magnus Pyke;

b Isaac Newton;

c Albert Einstein;

d Henry Ford?

8 Who was responsible for initially setting out the law of gravity:

a Michael Faraday;

b Isaac Newton;

c Albert Einstein;

d Charles Darwin?

9 Which of the following best illustrates Newton's Third Law of Motion, that for every action there is an equal and opposite reaction:

a it is easier to stop a tennis ball in your hand than a cricket ball;

b in a jet engine the force pushing back behind the engine propels it forward;

c every object remains in motion or stays motionless;

d less force is required to stop a heavy object than a lighter one?

10 The main discovery that we associate with Charles Darwin was:

a the discovery of white light;

b modern approaches to genetic modification of crops;

c the origin of species by descent with modification;

d the classification of bird life into different species?

11 Darwin's work indicated that:

a all species are gradually eliminated as they fail to adapt to their environment;

b birds with long, pointed beaks are always superior to ones with shorter beaks;

c species are modified during descent, in order to adapt to their environment;

d species found in one environment will be practically identical to those found in other environments.

12 We associate Albert Einstein with:

a the general theory of relativity;

b the discovery of the principal of gravity;

c the evolution of the species;

d experiments on electro-magnetism.

13 Einstein's formula $E = mc^2$ provided important background work in the development of:

a the nuclear bomb;

b the transistor radio;

c the dynamo;

d the internal combustion engine.

14 Which of the following is not a good example of the standardization process in car design:

a placing the hand break in a set location;.

b customizing vehicles to meet individual needs;

c everyone having to drive on the same side of the road;

d placing the accelerator, clutch and break pedals in the same order?

15 Which of the following means of communication reached a global audience of 50 million people in the shortest period of time:

a television;

b postal service;

c radio;

d internet?

Here are some more general questions.

1 Does science help us to get nearer the truth?

2 Have scientists like Newton and Einstein been able to unlock some of the secrets of the universe?

3 Do you think that work on such things as evolution, gravity, and relativity have helped us to better understand how the whole process of nature fits together – or does it just give us a partial view?

4 What is the relative importance of scientists and technologists?

5 What is the role that technology plays in our lives?

6 Which is more important to you – scientific discovery or technological achievement?

7 Do science and technology help us to progress? Are there situations in which they have the opposite effect?

4

Moral responsibility in science and technology

The distance between good and evil is as fine as the wing of a butterfly; in that between distance lies everything and nothing!

Ethical issues involve questions of morality but there is a fine line between what is good for mankind and what is harmful.

Genetic engineering is a good example of a moral issue relating to science and technological development. Strong ethical concerns are voiced about genetic engineering in the modern world, particularly with regard to:

- Plants – because they are at the heart of the food chain. The danger is that if modified crops harm natural crops and existing life forms, then we could rapidly find ourselves with a ravaged planet and a diminishing foodstore.

- Humans and animals – because of the ethics of tampering with sentient beings. The most strongly voiced concerns relate to genetic engineering of human embryos.

When Dolly, the cloned sheep, first hit the headlines, the American President at the time, Bill Clinton, immediately asked for an ethical report and, throughout the world, governments, concerned citizens and scientists have been engaged in a dialogue about new biological initiatives.

Questions

1 Do you think that, if genetic engineering leads to more disease-resistant species, it is a good or bad thing?

2 Do you believe that there is a hierarchy of ethical concern about genetic modification with plant modification being the least serious, followed by animals, and finally human embryos?

3 Is there a dividing line between what is ethically acceptable in scientific investigation and what is unacceptable?

key terms

ethics

Sets of moral principles.

genetic engineering

The deliberate modification of the characters of an organism by the manipulation of the genetic material.

sentient being

Being with sensory feelings such as touch, sight, smell and hearing.

cloning

Creating a person or thing that is identical with another, usually from the asexual production of cells from one stock or ancestor.

Scientific and technological developments have the power to transform the lives of all of us for the better, for example:

- scientific research into causes of illness and disease;

- medicine and drugs to ease the suffering of cancer patients;

- the development of cures for AIDS;

- the development of modern hospitals and emergency services;

- scientific research into the physical properties of materials;

- the development of new types of building materials to provide affordable housing;

- the development of new innovations in household products such as non-stick pans, which were a by-product of the space programme;

- scientific research into alternative renewable fuel sources;
- the development of cars that are not driven by petrol but, for example, by electric batteries, and so forth.

inoculating against smallpox

Smallpox is an acute contagious disease, with fever and postules, leaving permanent scars. The development of smallpox vaccine and other vaccines provides us with an excellent example of the way in which scientific investigation, coupled with the technological development of mass-produced vaccinations, has enabled us to live safer and hence better lives.

Edward Jenner (1749–1823), a native of Gloucestershire, took an interest in smallpox when he first began to hear local stories about immunity to this disease. He had heard that anyone infected with cowpox was immune to the deadlier smallpox. This was a belief that was strongly held by country people.

However, the idea of using an animal disease to combat a human one was regarded suspiciously by many people. Jenner's research led him to the conclusion that the discharge from a cowpox sore could be used for inoculation provided that it was taken at the right stage of the development of the disease in the cow or the human infected with smallpox.

To verify his belief he needed to test this out on a human being. If this had proved to be wrong then he would immediately have faced widespread criticism and a probable prison sentence.

In April 1796 he was sure of his belief, and using material obtained from the sores on a milkmaid's hands he inoculated a boy named Phipps in the arm. Immediately the boy developed cowpox but quickly recovered. Later, Phipps was injected with smallpox but produced no symptoms of the disease.

Jenner felt he had the proof to proceed and two years later published his findings. At first there was widespread criticism of his approach of using an animal vaccine (the word vaccine comes from the Latin word *vacca,* which means cow). However, the practice of vaccination quickly took off across Europe and America. It was a much safer method than inoculating a patient with smallpox.

However, at that date no one had a clear understanding of how the vaccine worked. Seventy years later, Louis Pasteur began a set of tests applying Jenner's method of using a less dangerous substance to inoculate against a more deadly one.

He needed a method of obtaining bacteria to use in the inoculation process. In 1880 he came across a case where a culture of cholera had become less virulent over time. Using this clue, by growing and filtering bacteria taken from animals, he was able to discover both a vaccine against anthrax and, in 1881, against rabies, which affects dogs and also humans who have either been bitten or been in close contact with them.

Vaccines were soon developed against tetanus and diphtheria. Today, modern technological processes are used to manufacture, preserve and distribute vast quantities of vaccines across the world, and some of the world's diseases have been eradicated. For example, smallpox, which was one of the most evil of all illnesses, killing millions of people and disfiguring countless others, has been banished from the world in recent years, with just some specimens being kept in research laboratories in case they are needed in the future. This has led to widespread fears that these bacteria could find their way into the wrong hands and be used for biological warfare.

So just as scientific and technological development makes us better off it also provides threats to our very existence – for example from biological warfare and from the production of items that involve cancer-threatening by-products.

Scientists and technologists face tremendous moral pressures. They need to make responsible choices, and consider the possible consequences of their actions. Nowhere is this more true than in the case of genetic modification of plants and animals, including humans.

■ Genetic engineering of plants

The subject of genetic engineering has been a particularly prominent area of debate in recent years and is useful as a basis for discussion of the moral responsibility of science and technology. The following materials are therefore designed to give you some brief background information about genetics before going on to identify issues related to the moral responsibilities of scientists and technologists in this field.

One of the most sensitive issues is the question of whether artificially developed microbes and plants, produced by genetic engineering, should be released into the environment. Traditional crop-breeding involves first seeking out a wild disease-resistant variety of the crop and then crossing this wild variety with a cultivated plant.

Wild strain of wheat that is disease resistant + Cultivated wheat = Hybrid wheat (disease resistant)

It is necessary to grow several generations of the hybrid crop in order to remove characteristics of the wild strain that are undesirable.

In contrast, genetic engineering of crops involves breeders taking a gene that is desired from a plant and then inserting this directly into a crop plant. This is not an easy process particularly for plants known as monocotyledons, from which most foodstuffs are grown – for example wheat, corn and rice.

However, in the late 1980s dramatic breakthroughs in this science were made in Germany where researchers injected solutions of genes into young buds on corn plants. When the flowers formed, plants that had been treated were cross-fertilized by each other. The purpose of this was to enable the injected deoxyribonucleic acid (DNA) to find its way into the reproductive cells, the pollen and ova of the flowers and thus into the future generations of the crop variety. Initially this only happened in a minority of cases, but with further research the process was developed into the much more exact science of genetic modification of plants with which we are familiar today. New varieties of crops are much more disease resistant and give higher yields than in the past. Moreover, crops have been 'designed' to cope with much more difficult weather conditions, with the possibility of enabling crop production in areas where it was previously impossible.

There are a number of criticisms levelled at genetic engineering of plants, including:

- Existing plants have developed over millions of years, in response to natural conditions through a process of natural selection. To tamper with this is to tamper with nature.

- There is no way to protect existing plants from newly planted genetically modified crops. New strains of crops germinate neighbouring fields and the wind can cause them to affect crops at considerable distances.

- Huge agricultural businesses are forcing genetically modified crops on the world, particularly on poorer, developing countries. Instead of having hundreds of varieties of rice we are moving to fewer and fewer strains.

- By reducing variation we are putting ourselves in peril. Having a broad variety means that plants as a whole are far more likely to resist disease and natural disaster. Concentrating on a few genetically modified strains is a far more risky process.

There have been widespread protests against genetically modified crops across the globe – with protesters seeking to raise public awareness, for example by destroying genetically modified crops in the fields where they have been planted.

Much of the research in crop breeding in recent years has been carried out by researchers working for large agricultural businesses. These companies plough large sums of money into these developments and they feel that they should receive the bulk of the rewards stemming from this research.

analyse
this

Is it ethical for giant companies to gain the exclusive rights to the genetic composition of products like rice? Read through the case study below and then answer the questions that follow it.

It is a basic entitlement for all people to receive enough food to enable them to live meaningful and fulfilling lives. However, currently, large numbers of people are not receiving this entitlement and it seems that this is in some measure our fault.

In June 2002 the United Nation's World Food Programme warned that nearly 13 million people in southern Africa faced famine by the end of the year as a result of drought, floods and political upheaval which had nearly halved grain production.

We in the West are able to enjoy high living standards, often at the expense of the developing world. We are able to buy more foodstuffs, pushing up the price, and thus making them inaccessible to people in the developing world. Even worse, we are currently buying up the exclusive rights to detailed knowledge about food products that for many years have been the staple products of the developing world.

Syngenta announced in 2001 that it had completed a draft map of the rice genome and wanted to publish the finished map in *Science* and so claim the scientific priority that comes with publication in a prestigious journal.

However, *Science* and Syngenta are understood to have come to an agreement that allows the company to retain the raw data – effectively the detailed DNA sequence of the rice plant – so it can store the information in a commercial database over which the company will have control.

Some of the most prominent specialists in the field of genetics, such as Bob Waterston of Washington University in St Louis; David Botstein of Stanford University in California; Michael Ashburner of Cambridge University; and Sir John Sulston of the Sanger Centre in Cambridge, signed a letter to *Science*. In it they said that a similar deal the previous year, which allowed the biotechnology company Celera to store its sequence of the human genome on its private database rather than having it published in a publicly available biotechnology database called GenBank, was highly damaging to the open tradition of science. 'At that time we, and many other colleagues, expressed dismay at this action, because of the absolute necessity for genomic research of having all of the public sequence data available from one place', the scientists wrote. 'We are happy to share with you now the arguments then made, and they remain as valid now as then, as to why deposition of sequence data in the Genetic Bank is so important for the scientific community at large', they stated.

The authors of the letter urged the editorial board of *Science* to change the journal's policy and bring it in line with the accepted norms in the field.

The scientists opposed to the arrangement included British Nobel laureates Sir Paul Nurse and Sir Aaron King. Sir Aaron said that the Syngenta plan 'went against the ethics of scientific research. It's to do with the ethics of publication. The tradition is to publish and tell the world. If you do not publish then you cannot claim credit.'

Questions

1 What do you understand by 'the open tradition of science'? Give an example of how this might work out in practice.

2 Are you in favour of, or opposed to, this open tradition?

3 In which fields are the open tradition most important? Why?

4 Is it ethical to hold back scientific discoveries? Explain your answer.

5 Can you think of areas in which there might not be an open tradition? Why?

6 What is your view of business organizations that seek to limit access to scientific information? Why might they seek to withhold this information?

■ Human genetics

The issue of genetic engineering of plants is highly controversial, but there is even more controversy in relation to work that is being carried out into animal cloning, and still more in relation to experimentation with people.

Before looking at the controversy in this area, we first need to examine some of the science associated with human genetics.

Life is a four-letter word

In the English language, life is definitely spelled L, I, F, E. However, to a geneticist, the letters that spell life are the four letters A, C, G and T. These letters are shorthand names for the four different kinds of chemical building blocks that are the basis for every living thing. The 'A' stands for adenine, the 'C' for focytosine, the 'D' for quanine, and the 'T' for thymine. They are all nucleotides, which means that they are all compounds formed from sugar, phosphates and nitrogen. Different combinations of these nucleotides make up the two separate strands of DNA, the two strands winding around each other to form the famous double helix. Genes are linear sections of this helix.

You can describe DNA as a book of instructions (the genes) on how to create a body and make it work. The book is written using only those four letters A, C, G and T but it is vast. For instance, in humans the book contains enough information to fill 5000 volumes of the *Encyclopaedia*

We share 90% of our DNA with the mouse

key terms

genome

Is a word formed from 'gene' and 'chromosome'.

chromosome

Is formed from the Greek words for colour (chroma) and body (soma) and is so-named because a chromosome res-ponds to certain dyes that make it more visible – although not very.

Britannica. Everything alive, every worm, woodpecker, daisy, lion, shark, oak tree and human being, including you, and every bacterium and every virus, in fact everything that has life, owes that life and its continuing existence to the four nucleotides and the combinations they make in DNA. We really are all brothers and sisters under the skin. We share 90 per cent of our DNA with the mouse, and more than a third with the nematode worm. Speaking in genetic terms only, even bacteria are our relations.

So how do these nucleotides – these four letters of life – operate? This is where it becomes a little more complicated.

Every human body consists of approximately 1000 million cells, most of them less than a tenth of a millimetre in width. Each cell has a nucleus and inside each nucleus there are two complete human genomes – a 'genome' is the full set of the 100 000 or so human genes arranged on 23 chromosomes. So each cell has 23 paired chromosomes (at least that is the number in a human genome – some species have fewer, some more; chimpanzees, for instance, have 24). Some cells contain only one genome. These are the egg cells in a female body and the sperm cells in a male body. The reason is that when the winning sperm enters the egg, the resultant fertilized egg – now the foetus – contains the necessary pair of genomes and no more. Red blood cells contain no genomes at all.

Under a microscope a chromosome appears as a long thread with the genes strung along it. If you could spread out in line all the chromosomes in a single cell, they would stretch to about two metres. If you could lay out all the chromosomes in your body they would stretch for about 100 billion miles.

In those cells (nearly all of them) that have two genomes, one comes from your father, the other from your mother. Each of the chromosomes in the genome from one parent is a kind of pair to one of the chromosomes in the genomes from the other. Sometimes there is a clash between the genes in one of the pairs. For instance, one gene on a chromosome inherited from your father might predispose you to having brown eyes. A corresponding gene from your mother's side might predispose you to having blue eyes. Whether your eyes turn out to be brown or blue depends on which of those two genes is the dominant and which the recessive (the 'brown' gene is usually the dominant).

The smallest human chromosome, arbitrarily dubbed number 21, is one of very few that can be present in a viable human body in three copies rather than two. If an unborn baby has three of virtually any other chromosome it is unlikely to be born alive and, if it is, it will certainly die within a few days. However, babies with three of chromosome 21 may live happy healthy lives for many years. They have Down's syndrome. Typically they have plump cheerful faces, narrow eyes, they are not very tall and they are mentally retarded. Generally they will die early, often of a form of Alzheimer's disease. Mothers-to-be are now generally able to have screening tests that will determine whether the foetus carries this extra chromosome or not.

The genes are the result of the combination of the four nucleotides into a series of three-letter sequences (call them 'words' for the sake of convenience). Each gene is a 'sentence' composed of words in a specific order and each gene has a specific function. It contributes to the making of a specific kind of protein – which can be an enzyme (to help with digestion for instance), an antibody (to combat disease) or a receptor protein in the brain (to help you think). Proteins make up most of our bodies and control all the chemical processes inside the cell, turning them off and on as required for the normal functioning of the whole organism. The DNA molecules – and hence each individual gene – have another very special property. They find it easy to replicate themselves. This is just as well, or you would not be here. When you were first conceived, you were no more than a single cell, with the two genomes stored in its nucleus. You now have trillions of cells. Replication of the genome (give or take a few mutations – although these can be fatal to the total organism) is completely accurate, which is why daisies continue to be daisies and produce more daisies. Likewise with flies, human beings and every other living thing.

The double helix

The foundation of modern genetics was laid in 1953 by two comparatively young scientists working at Cambridge University – the American James Watson and the Englishman Francis Crick. They reported that genetic material on the chromosomes – the genes – was encoded on the DNA molecule, the famous double helix. Since then, growth in our understanding of our genetic makeup has accelerated phenomenally, so much so that we can count ourselves lucky to be alive at a time when it has become possible to identify and chart each of the 100 000 genes on the human genome. The work of identification has been carried out on both sides of the Atlantic but most prominently at the Wellcome Trust's Sanger Centre in Cambridge. Today, you are able to obtain a 'first draft' of the complete genetic code on the internet.

Questions

1   What is the significance of the double helix?

2   In the context of the document, what can worms, oak trees, daisies and human beings be said to share in common?

3   Where do the genomes in the cells in your body originate from?

4   Why is it important for genes to replicate themselves?

analyse
this

potential rewards

The potential rewards of mapping the human genome are enormous and the implications are thought provoking. When we each know our genetic make-up in accurate detail we will have a clear insight into our medical destiny – whether we are likely to develop this or that disease. This knowledge may be highly encouraging or deeply depressing. It might also tempt us to forget that our environment, our will power and such intangible and unscientific concepts as spirit and soul are also powerful determinants of our destiny. Genes are not the be all and end all. Less controversially, it can be said that by understanding much more fully the influence that genes have on such human disasters as cancer, cystic fibrosis and Alzheimer's disease, we will be able to devise new and more effective treatments and possibly cures. Moreover, DNA testing has a great range of other practical benefits to offer – for example, in forensic science (helping to identify criminals and bringing them to justice) and in archaeology.

Question

Are you in favour of scientists mapping out the genetic make-up of humans? Explain your answer.

■ Cloning – and the redesign of humans and other animals

Dolly the cloned sheep who died in 2003

The revolution in our knowledge of genetics raises a number of other problems about the use and possible abuse of so-called 'genetic engineering'. Perhaps the ultimate use of this technique is 'cloning'. Dolly the sheep, the first mammal to be cloned from an adult cell, was an exact genetic replica of her mother. Are we to 'progress' to cloning human beings?

The other highly publicized form of genetic engineering is genetic modification (GM). This is based on the fact that with the help of certain bacterial enzymes, DNA can be cut into small fragments and joined together again in another combination with or without the addition of DNA from other species. The genetic modification of plants to increase yields and reduce disease has provoked special controversy, with shouting matches between those who are for and against. One possible attitude to take is that it is impossible to un-invent something. Genetic modification has been achieved. It must now be controlled and the debate about how to do this is not primarily scientific.

These issues raise the question of moral responsibility. If morality involves distinguishing between what is 'right' and 'wrong' then moral responsibility involves making the 'right' decisions.

There are different ways of thinking about morality in this context. One view of morality might be based on a religious belief – that God has ordained the nature of life on earth. Tampering with the makeup of animals and people is therefore morally irresponsible.

However, opponents of this view would argue that plant and animal breeders have always sought to provide better strains of crops and creatures.

An alternative view of moral responsibility is that we have a duty to make life better for our children and for future generations. If we can breed humans that are stronger, and more disease resistant, and if we can increase food supplies, for example by developing cows that produce more milk and meat, then we are acting in a socially responsible way.

analyse
this

Discuss the following question. What do you see as being 'morally responsible' in terms of genetic modification or plants and animals?

analyse
this

the triumph of genetic modification?

Read through the material below, which suggests that it may be morally responsible to 'make better human beings', and then give your own view. The following is an outline of a review of a book with the title *Redesigning Humans*, by Gregory Stock. The review was written by Brenda Maddox and appeared in the *Guardian Review* on 1 June 2002.

Gregory Stock looks at gene manipulation and artificial reproduction and sees hope, health and challenge. If we can make better human beings, why not do it? Mother Nature has not been particularly kind: 'Brutal decay lies in store for each of us lucky enough to reach it.' Postponing the blighting afflictions – stroke, cancer, Alzheimer's – reducing infertility, preventing birth defects; all these can hardly be called inhumane.

Stock's book has much to offer those inclined to believe that the end of the world is not yet nigh. He directs (at the medical school of UCLA, in America) a programme

on the impact of new technologies on human society. He musters evidence that the worst may be behind us. Nuclear annihilation, forced sterilisation and eugenics or 'race hygiene', are 20th century scientific nightmares that have retreated rather than advanced. And 'playing God' is as old as harnessing fire, carving stone tools, rotating crops or flying aircraft.

Piglets with jellyfish genes

He sees the worst fears are unrealistic – such as the creation of a new breed, a race distinct from ordinary mortals. Centuries of dog-breeding, he points out, have not altered the canine species. Designer babies also are unlikely. All the new techniques carry inherent risks that will deter those who would drastically alter genes.

The coming genetic revolution in Stock's view, will be wary of unintended consequences, and will advance in slow, reversible steps. He cites China's gender imbalance, the unforeseen corollary of its one-child policy. In a generation this anomaly will disappear as did the surplus of females following the slaughter of the First World War. As for cloning, twins are living proof that identical genes do not mean identical personality.

A genetically modified feather-free chicken

The fearful should recognise that in some ways, the future has already arrived. In vitro fertilisation is accepted, as is 'pre-implantation diagnosis' – selecting among laboratory-created embryos to find one free of, say, cystic fibrosis. So too is amniocentesis, to look for Down's syndrome. Still to be developed for medical use is gene alteration, the insertion of artificial chromosomes and reproductive cloning. In every case, in Stock's eyes the advantages outweigh the risks.

The true challenge is to find a form of enforceable, internationally accepted regulation that will focus on real and present problems, not on future, imagined ones. It may be desirable to test embryos with a view

A mouse with a human ear growing from its back

to eliminating the risk of severe disability, but should such tests be compulsory? Should a subsequent abortion? If parental choice is to be respected, ought deaf parents be allowed to choose to have deaf children? With both lifespan and fertility lengthening dramatically, perhaps there should be a legal age limit for reproduction for women. And for men too?

Stock's worry is that Europe, mindful of bans in Germany and France against any laboratory work that may lead to modification of the human gene pool, will pull out of the world's most exciting scientific endeavour.

Questions

1 How does Gregory Stock think that genetic engineering and artificial reproduction can help us fight 'brutal decay'?

2 Explain one other reason given by Stock to argue that genetic engineering should not be feared.

3 What does Stock see as being the key challenge in making genetic engineering safe and appropriate?

4 Take one of his views that you strongly agree or disagree with. Explain why you agree or disagree with this view.

5 Do you agree that Stock is taking a morally responsible view? Explain your opinion.

6 What arguments might an opponent of Stock put forward to contradict Stock's view?

analyse this

moral responsibility and finding a potential cure for AIDS

The charts below appeared in *The Times* newspaper on 15 July 2002.

Estimated adults living with HIV/AIDS in Africa

Country	Total adults (aged 15–49) (00's)	Percentage of total adult population
Botswana	2,800	35.80
Burkina Faso	3,300	6.44
Burundi	3,400	11.32

Cameroon	5,200	7.73
Central African Republic	2,300	13.84
Congo	820	6.43
Cote d'Ivoire	7,300	10.76
Dem. Republic of Congo	11,000	5.07
Djibouti	350	11.75
Ethiopia	29,000	10.63
Gabon	220	4.16
Gambia	120	1.95
Ghana	3,300	3.60
Kenya	20,000	13.95
Lesotho	2,400	23.57
Malawi	7,600	15.96
Mozambique	11,000	13.22
Namibia	1,500	19.54
Nigeria	26,000	5.06
Rwanda	3,700	11.21
Sierra Leone	650	2.99
South Africa	41,000	19.94
Swaziland	1,200	25.25
Togo	1,200	5.98
Uganda	7,700	8.30
United Rep. of Tanzania	12,000	8.09
Zambia	8,300	19.95
Zimbabwe	14,000	25.06
Total	**234,442**	**8**

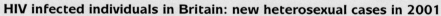

HIV infected individuals in Britain: new heterosexual cases in 2001

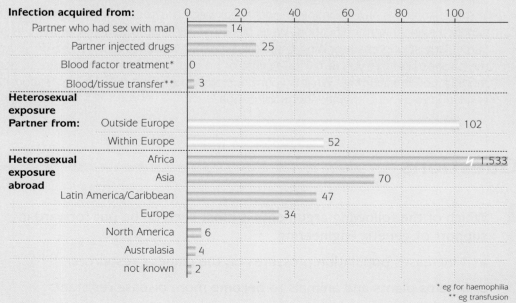

Infection acquired from:		
Partner who had sex with man	14
Partner injected drugs	25
Blood factor treatment*	0
Blood/tissue transfer**	3
Heterosexual exposure Partner from: Outside Europe	102
Within Europe	52
Heterosexual exposure abroad Africa	1,533
Asia	70
Latin America/Caribbean	47
Europe	34
North America	6
Australasia	4
not known	2

* eg for haemophilia
** eg transfusion

Questions

1 What evidence is provided that AIDS is a serious problem for Britain? Give statistics that back up your claim.

2 Where else is AIDS a problem according to the charts? How serious a problem is it in these countries? Give evidence to back up your claim.

At the same time as this information was widely publicized it was also reported that a human gene that can protect the body against infection with HIV had been identified by a team of scientists. The scientists discovered that the gene, which is named CEM15, confers natural resistance to HIV but is normally knocked out by a small protein in the virus called virion infectivity factor (Vif). The findings suggest a promising new approach towards treating and preventing HIV. If a drug can be designed to neutralize the Vif protein, it would allow CEM15 to work normally, stopping HIV from infecting and replicating in human cells.

3 Are you in favour of scientist carrying out this research that would involve modifying the way that genes operate in the human body?

4 Why would you support/not support such research?

5 Is it a moral responsibility of scientists and technologists to find a cure for AIDS?

analyse this

In this chapter we have examined evidence showing the good and the bad things about genetic engineering/modification. What pieces of evidence would you support as being particularly strong in supporting genetic engineering/modification? Where do you think the balance lies? Are you in favour/against or do you have mixed feelings about genetic modification/engineering? What is your understanding of the term 'moral responsibility' in relation to genetic engineering/modification?

Questions

1 Which of the following arguments is most likely to be put forward in support of genetic engineering:

a it increases population pressures on the planet's resources;

b it helps plants and animals to become more disease resistant;

c it reduces the number of species required on the earth;

d it creates a master race of super species that are scientist designed?

2 Edward Jenner's development of a cowpox vaccine was originally founded on:

a tales that he had heard from country people;

b his own original development of theory;

c a chance scientific experiment in the laboratory;

d copying the work of other leading scientists.

3 Jenner's first inoculation of his patient Phipps was with:

a living smallpox material;

b material from the sores on a milkmaid's hands;

c an artificial vaccine created in the laboratory;

d live anthrax cells.

4 Louis Pasteur built on Jenner's work by using:

a highly virulent cultures of cholera;

b non-animal based artificial vaccines;

c animal bacteria that had been filtered to become less virulent;

d more deadly substances to inoculate against less deadly ones.

5 Louis Pasteur developed vaccines for all of the following *except*:

a rabies;

b anthrax;

c smallpox;

d AIDS.

6 Genetically modifying crops involves:

a taking a gene from a desired plant and inserting it into others;

b crossing wild plants with cultivated ones;

c growing hybrids through cross-fertilization;

d searching for new species of plant life.

7 Which of the following is a benefit of the process of genetic modification of plants:

a genetically modified crops can harm existing natural plants;

    b successful varieties of plants are reducing the diversity of crops grown;

    c genetically modified plants often give greater crop yields;

    d genetic modification tampers with process of natural selection?

8 Which of the following is not one of the four building blocks of life:

    a A – adenine;

    b T – thymine;

    c G – glucose;

    d C – focytosine?

9 With which of the following do humans share 90 per cent of their DNA:

    a plants;

    b nematode worms;

    c mice;

    d bacteria?

10 How many chromosomes are human genes arranged on?

    a 2

    b 23

    c 24

    d 100 000.

11 How many genomes are there in red blood cells?

    a 0

    b 2

    c 23

    d 24.

12 Which of the following helps with the digestion process:

    a antibodies;

    b receptor proteins;

    c genomes;

    d enzymes?

13 The shape of the DNA molecule is typically:

    a a regular polygon;

b a double helix;

c a circle;

d a square.

14 Roughly how many genes are there in a human genome?

a 1

b 2

c 23

d 100 000.

15 The first mammal to be cloned from an adult cell was:

a a grain of wheat;

b a chimpanzee;

c a sheep;

d a human.

16 Which of the following is not a 'moral judgement' related to genetic engineering:

a a religious view that tampering with natural creatures is unacceptable;

b a view that manipulating genetics can improve human welfare;

c a statistical survey examining the improvement in species through cloning;

d a view that is totally opposed to any form of genetic modification?

Here are some more general questions for you to consider.

1 Which are you most in favour of/most opposed to – genetic modification of plants/crops, genetic modification of animals, or genetic modification of humans?

2 What is the relationship between ethics and genetic modification?

3 Are there any situations in which genetic modification is acceptable/unacceptable?

4 What are the benefits and drawbacks of genetic modification?

5

The characteristics of the sciences

Many scientists believe that the universe was formed by a 'big bang' and that the galaxies that make up the universe are moving apart over time. The galaxy of which the Earth is part is called the Milky Way.

Questions

1   Do you believe that the universe was started by a 'big bang'? Or do you think that there is a creator at work behind the universe and life?

2   What do you see as being the difference between a star and a planet?

3   Is the planet Earth different from other planets?

4   What is the principal source of energy for planet Earth?

5   Do you think that the division of Earth into continents and oceans always had the same pattern?

key terms

supernatural

A non-natural explanation that reveals some 'truth' about how nature operates, for example explaining an event in terms of the powers of a mystical godlike presence.

orbit

The curved course of a planet.

ellipse

A regular oval, traced by a point moving in a plane so that the sum of its distances from/ to other points is constant.

planet

A celestial body moving in an elliptical way around a star.

star

A large gaseous body, luminous in the night sky as a result of internal gaseous combustion.

In the modern world science is part of our everyday lives – from the treatment of disease to the generation of energy, and the manufacture of clothes and cosmetics, our lives are affected by the results of scientific research.

- Much of our entertainment and communications (cinema, television, mobile phones and so forth);

- Agriculture (the production of richer harvests, development of new crop varieties);

- Artificial materials that we use (synthetic carpets, curtains, clothes, sportswear and so forth),

all depend on using facts that scientists discovered.

When we refer to the 'scientific age' we refer to the application of science to technological development.

Underpinning all of these developments are scientific investigations in the fields of physics, chemistry and biology, which have helped us to gain a better understanding of fundamental issues, such as:

- the origin of the universe, space and matter;

- natural forces and the sources and forms of energy;

- the Earth's resources; and

- the nature of life on our planet.

The first three of these fundamental issues are the subject of this chapter, and the following chapter examines aspects of the nature of life.

■ The origins of the universe, space and matter

Early man sought supernatural explanations for existence on Earth, and identified a range of gods – for example gods of the harvest – who determined the best time for planting and needed to be appeased to ensure a rich crop. This search for supernatural explanations has continued right up to the present day; for example Christians use the Harvest Festival to

▶ space

The near-vacuum extending between the planets and stars, containing small amounts of gas and dust.

matter

That which has a mass and occupies space.

'big bang'

The explosion of dense matter thought to mark the start of the universe.

The Hubble Space Telescope

thank God for his bounty, and tribespeople in New Guinea created models of aeroplanes that they saw flying overhead and assumed to mark the presence of a beneficial deity.

One of the most significant points in the development of mankind was the realization that 'the universe is understandable'.

The ancient Greek astronomers realized that by observing the heavens and thinking carefully about what they saw, they could begin to understand some of the mysteries of the universe. For example, they developed ways of measuring the size of the Earth, and understood and were able to predict eclipses. Later, Galileo and Newton were to develop telescopes that were the forerunners of the highly sophisticated tools used by modern astronomers. For example, the Hubble Space Telescope orbits the Earth in space.

The Hubble Space Telescope can detect not only visible light but also ultraviolet and near-infrared light (which are difficult to detect on Earth because they are absorbed by the atmosphere). This telescope is large enough to be seen with the naked eye from Earth.

■ The solar system

The solar system is made up of the sun and all of the celestial bodies that orbit it, including:

- the Earth;
- the other eight planets;
- moons of the various planets.

The sun is a typical star. Its diameter is roughly a million miles and its surface temperature is about 55 000°C. The sun draws its energy from thermonuclear reactions occurring at its centre.

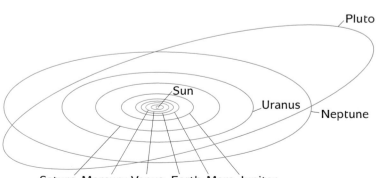

This diagram shows the orbits of the planets around the sun. Earth, Venus, Mercury and Mars are clustered close to the sun, with the five other planets much further away. On this scale the planets would not be visible as they would be smaller than a human hair.

Most of the planets have nearly circular orbits (Kepler discovered in the sixteenth century that they are actually ellipses). The eccentricity of a circle is zero and the orbits of most of the planets have eccentricities that are close to zero. The exceptions are Mercury and Pluto, which have non-circular orbal eceentricities. Pluto's orbit takes it nearer to the sun than does Neptune's. Fortunately, the orbits of these planets are such that they will never collide.

The planets orbit the sun in the same counterclockwise direction, and all lie in nearly the same plane.

Orbital characteristics of the planets are shown in the table below.

	Average distance from sun		Orbital period (years)
	Astronomical Units (AU)	**(10^6km)**	
Mercury	0.387	57.9	0.241
Venus	0.723	108.2	0.615
Earth	1.000	149.6	1.000
Mars	1.524	227.9	1.881
Jupiter	5.203	778.3	11.86
Saturn	9.555	1429.0	29.42
Uranus	19.22	2875.0	83.75
Neptune	30.11	4504.0	163.7
Pluto	39.54	5916.0	248.0

The physical characteristics of the planets are such that they naturally fall into two classes:

- Four inner planets, Earth, Venus, Mars and Mercury.
- Four outer planets, Jupiter, Saturn, Uranus and Neptune.

The inner planets are called terrestrial planets because they are similar to the Earth. They have hard rocky surfaces with mountains, volcanoes, craters and canyons. You could stand on the surface of any of these planets in a protective spacesuit.

The outer four planets are different. They are called the Jovian planets because they resemble Jupiter. You could not land a spacecraft on these planets because the materials of which they are made are mostly gaseous or liquid. The visible 'surface' features of a Jovian planet are actually cloud formations in the planet's atmosphere. Pluto is an exceptional case, being made up of ice and rock.

Physical characteristics of the planets

	Equatorial diameter (km)	Mass (Earth = 1)	(kg)	(Earth = 1)	Average density (kg/m³)
Mercury	4879	0.383	3202×10^{23}	0.055	5430
Venus	12104	0.949	4869×10^{24}	0.815	5240
Earth	12756	1.000	5974×10^{24}	1.000	5515
Mars	6794	0.533	6419×10^{23}	0.107	3940
Jupiter	142984	11.210	1899×10^{27}	317.830	1330
Saturn	120536	9.450	5685×10^{26}	95.160	700
Uranus	51118	4.010	8662×10^{25}	14.500	1300
Neptune	49528	3.888	1028×10^{26}	17.200	1760
Pluto	2302	0.180	1500×10^{22}	0.0025	1100

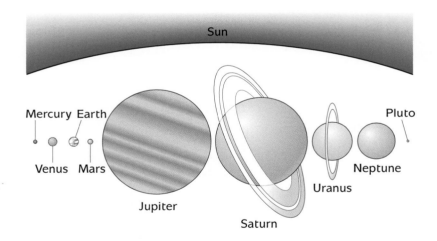

■ The origin of the universe, space and matter

One of the most important questions facing mankind is 'How did it all begin?' This leads on to other more philosophical questions such as: 'What is the purpose of life on Earth?' We will leave the second question for your speculation and we will focus on some of the latest lines of thinking about the origin of the universe.

Today we have far more information about the universe than ever before. In the early days speculation and scientific thinking were simply based on evidence from our own planet. Now we have far more evidence to draw on. From the 1960s onwards a series of unmanned spacecraft have visited and explored aspects of all the planets except Pluto. Remote 'eyes' have been used on spacecraft which have:

- brought rocks and space dust back from the moon;
- flown over Mercury's cratered surface;
- peered beneath Venus's poisonous clouds;
- discovered enormous craters and canyons on the surface of Mars;
- found active volcanoes on Jupiter;
- observed the rings of Saturn and Uranus close up;
- looked down on the active atmosphere of Neptune.

In the 1920s and 1930s scientists were able to work out how the sun creates energy through thermonuclear reactions that take place at its centre. It is the sun that creates the energy that enables life forms to exist on our planet. But how were the sun, other stars and the various planets created?

Stars are grouped into galaxies, which are of many different shapes and sizes. Our own galaxy is called the Milky Way, and it is made up of hundreds of billions of stars.

Evidence suggests that the universe began with what is called the big bang, which was at the beginning of time. Observations carried out by astronomers suggest that the universe is 'expanding' and that the galaxies that make up the universe are all moving away from each other.

Most astronomers currently think that the present phase of expansion began with all the matter in the universe exploding in one 'big bang'. The remaining question is whether the present expansion will continue forever, or whether it will stop and all the galaxies will then come back together for another 'big bang' and another expansion.

The universe has been expanding for billions of years. This means that in the past the matter in the universe must have been closer together and therefore denser than it is today. If we look far enough back in time we would arrive at a situation where the density of matter would be inconceivably high. This would have led to a 'big bang' – which created the universe.

The Hubble law of velocity shows how the universe is expanding. This law states that 'the recessional velocity of a galaxy is directly proportional to its distance from the Earth'.

This means that a galaxy twice as far way is receding from the Earth twice as fast – as one would expect in an expanding universe.

We can illustrate this by drawing a grid of parallel lines criss-crossing the universe. In the first illustration shown below, the gridlines are 100 mpc apart with five galaxies, shown as A, B, C, D and E, which we will assume lie at the intersection of the gridlines.

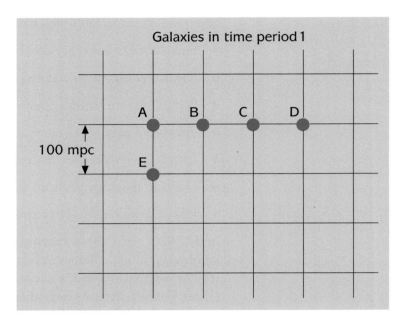

The second illustration shows a later time when the gridlines are 50 per cent further apart (150 mpc) and all the distances between galaxies are 50 per cent greater.

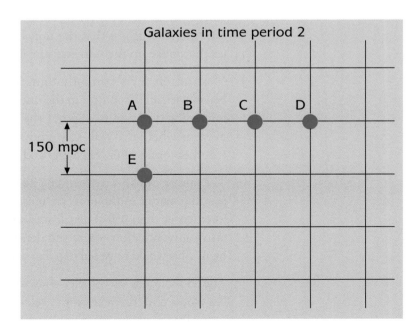

We can show how these galaxies have moved apart in a table that assumes that our own galaxy, the Milky Way, is galaxy A.

	Original distance (mpc)	Later distance (mpc)	Change in distance (mpc)
Milky Way – B	100	150	50
Milky Way – C	200	300	100
Milky Way – D	300	450	150
Milky Way – E	100	150	50

■ The nature of matter

All of the objects in the universe – the stars, planets, rocks, air, water and you and I – are made up of matter, which we have defined as something that occupies space.

Matter may exist in three states – gas, liquid and solid – and transformations from one state to another may occur under appropriate conditions of pressure and temperature. For example, a solid or gas could evaporate to form a liquid.

Different types of matter can vary in colour, hardness, mass, density and temperature and some types of matter react chemically when they come in contact with other types.

Matter exerts a gravitational pull on other objects and is, in turn, attracted by them. Matter has inertia – that is, if at rest, it tends to remain in a state of rest and if in motion it tends to resist any change in this motion.

Atoms are the basic units that make up matter, and atoms themselves are divisible into a large number of still smaller units. Atoms are in constant motion at all temperatures above absolute zero. The rate of motion is more rapid at higher temperatures.

A solid tends to keep its shape and volume because the atoms in it are in contact with one another and vibrate back and forth in fixed positions within a rigid, three-dimensional pattern.

A liquid has a certain volume but is shaped by its container; its atoms are in contact, but they are not part of a rigid pattern.

A gas diffuses throughout the container that shapes it. The atoms in a gas may be combined into molecules, but the molecules are in motion and are spaced relatively far apart. As a result gases are readily compressed, unlike solids and liquids.

Gas pressure results from the impacts of moving molecules against objects. The pressure is greater at high temperatures and pressures, where molecular motion is more rapid, impacts are more powerful, and more molecules occur within a unit volume.

A solid can be changed into a liquid (melting) if temperatures are increased enough. A gas condenses into a liquid if temperatures are decreased enough and pressures are increased.

Between 98 per cent and 99 per cent of all of the matter in the universe consists of two gases, hydrogen and helium.

Questions

1 Which of the following is most likely to be considered a supernatural explanation of the origin of the universe?

a An explanation based on gathering of scientific evidence.

b A belief based on religious conviction in God's creation of nature.

c A theory based on the collection of facts about an expanding universe.

d A researched account based on detailed gathering of relevant data.

2 Which of the following is a star:

a Pluto;

b Earth;

c Venus;

d the Sun?

3 Which of the following has the least circular orbit:

a Mercury;

b Venus;

c Earth;

d Mars?

4 Which of the following is not a terrestrial planet:

a Venus;

b Mercury;

c Earth;

d Neptune?

5 Which of the following is not a Jovian planet:

a Earth;

b Jupiter;

c Saturn;

d Uranus?

6 Which of the following planets is made of ice and rock:

a Jupiter;

b Uranus;

c Saturn;

d Pluto?

7 Which is the least dense planet:

a Uranus;

b Mercury;

c Saturn;

d Earth?

8 Which of the following planets has the greatest equatorial diameter:

a Uranus;

b Neptune;

c Earth;

d Jupiter?

9 Which of the following planets has the greatest mass:

a Pluto;

b Venus;

c Earth;

d Jupiter?

10 Which planet is nearest to the sun:

a Mercury;

b Pluto;

c Earth;

d Uranus?

11 Which planet takes longest to orbit around the sun:

a Earth;

b Venus;

c Mercury;

d Pluto?

12 Of which of the following is the Earth *not* a part:

a the Milky Way;

b the Solar System;

c the terrestrial planets;

d the Jovian planets?

13 What is the name for a cluster of hundreds of billions of stars:

a a black hole;

b a galaxy;

c a planet;

d a big bang?

14 If the universe is expanding then:

a Earth is getting bigger;

b the sun is getting hotter;

c galaxies are moving away from each other;

d it will become easier to travel to distant parts of the universe.

15 If the 'big bang' theory is accurate then:

a the universe is currently contracting;

b in the past the universe must have been denser than today;

c in the past the universe was more spread out than today;

d the further a galaxy is away from Earth the slower it is receding from Earth.

16 What are the basic units that make up matter:

a liquids;

b motion;

c atoms;

d solids?

17 The rate of motion of atoms:

   a is always constant;

   b is greater at lower temperatures;

   c is more rapid at higher temperatures;

   d does not vary with temperature.

18 Which of the following is true?

   a Atoms that make up solids do not keep fixed positions.

   b The atoms of a liquid are not part of a rigid pattern.

   c A gas shapes the container that it is contained in.

   d Gas pressure is greater at lower temperatures.

19 About 98 per cent to 99 per cent of the matter in the universe consists of:

   a oxygen;

   b carbon;

   c hydrogen and helium;

   d carbon dioxide and helium.

key terms

atmosphere

The envelope of gases surrounding the Earth.

hydrosphere

The waters of the Earth's surface.

evaporation

Turn from solid or liquid into vapour.

erosion

Wearing away. ▶

■ Earth and its resources

Geology (the word deriving from the Greek for Earth science) is concerned with the Earth – its origin, surface features, interior and physical conditions – with the organisms that once inhabited Earth, and with the countless changes that have occurred in all of these during the millennia that planet Earth has orbited the sun.

The study of geology helps us to understand various natural forces and natural features such as:

● geysers;

● earthquakes;

● volcanoes;

● waterfalls;

● landslides,

and many other things. As well as these exciting natural phenomena, geology also tells us more about our planet Earth.

▶ **glaciers**

Slowly moving mass or river of ice formed by the accumulation and compacting of snow on mountains or near the poles.

rift valley

A steep-sided valley formed by subsidence of the Earth's crust between nearly parallel faults.

specific gravity

Relative density.

Key facts about Earth

● It is about 4.6 billion years old.

● It is nearly spherical in shape, slightly flattened at the poles and bulging at the equator.

● It rotates through 360° once every 23 hours and 56 minutes.

● It revolves around the sun once in every 365 and a quarter days.

● It has a circumference of about 25 000 miles.

● The specific gravity of the Earth as a whole is about 5.5 – an average sample contains 5.5 times as much matter as does an equal volume of water. As this is about double the specific gravity of rocks at the Earth's surface, materials in its interior must be much more dense.

The Earth has an atmosphere unlike, for example, the moon. The fact that the Earth has an atmosphere helps to explain many of its distinguishing natural features. For example, there is wind, and wind causes erosion by blowing sand grains and smaller particles against rocks. Wind also produce waves and sea currents, which then erode shorelines. The evaporation of water from the oceans by solar energy leads to the formation of clouds that are transported inland to form rain, which subsequently returns to the seas. In addition, atmospheric gases react chemically with rocks to create further erosion.

The hydrosphere consists of the Earth's waters – with oceans submerging about 71 per cent of the Earth's surface. Large quantities of water are contained at the poles in the form of frozen glaciers – which, if they were to melt in their entirety, would completely cover the land.

Divisions of the Earth

The Earth is made up of three main divisions.

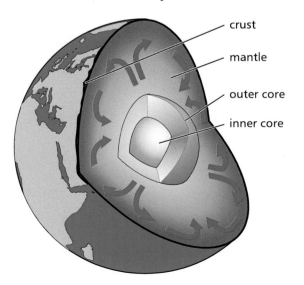

crust

mantle

outer core

inner core

1. Currents rise beneath mid-ocean ridge, causing ocean floor to spread apart and continue to drift.

2. Where currents descend they may push against continental plates and form coastal banks and deep sea trenches.

The *core* is the heart of the Earth and is principally made up of iron. There are two parts to the core:

● an inner part that seems to be solid;

● an outer part that appears to be fluid.

The *mantle* makes up about 84 per cent of the volume of the Earth. The Earth's core only makes up a very small part of the Earth as a whole. It is much thicker (about six times) beneath the continents than beneath the oceans. It is much thicker than average beneath the mountain belts. The Earth's surface has three main units:

● continents;

● ocean basins;

● mid-ocean ridges.

The origin of continents, oceans and mid-ocean ranges

Recent theory suggests that oceanic crust may be forming today at a mid-ocean ridge because material from the mantle underneath moves upward into its crest, along which a zone of tension and rift valleys is found. The newly formed crust then spreads laterally away from the ridge crest, making room for additional material from the mantle in a process that may have been going on for millions of years. Eventually, this young ocean

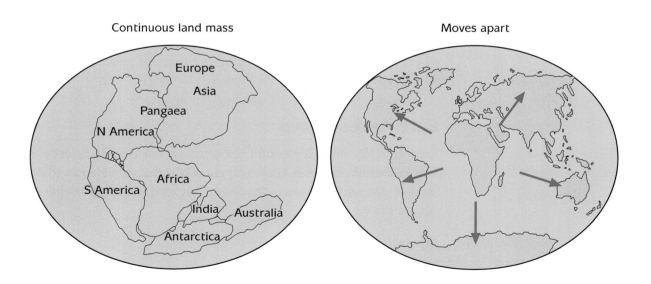

floor arrives at a deep-sea trench and descends to be assimilated by the upper mantle.

If this view is correct, then the continents are drifting apart and the ocean beds are relatively young features.

Minerals and rocks in the Earth's surface

If you dig in your garden, beneath the Earth you will eventually come across a layer of rock that is referred to as the bedrock. Man only has access to minerals that lie in the very thin outer part of the Earth's crust – the deepest mines only go about 2 miles down, and the deepest wells about 5 miles.

Chemical analysis has been carried out of the various rock types in the outer 10 miles of the Earth's surface and the various elements contained. Eight elements make up 98 per cent of the weight of this zone. These elements are:

- oxygen;
- silicon;
- aluminium;
- iron;
- calcium;
- sodium;
- potassium; and
- magnesium.

Of these eight elements, oxygen and silicon combined as silica make up about three-quarters of the total. Although oxygen only makes up about 47 per cent of the 10-mile zone by weight, it actually accounts for about 93 per cent of the volume.

Earth's resources

Earth provides us with plentiful resources: the air that we breathe, the water we drink, minerals, rocks and chemicals that provide us with millions of different substances involved with food, clothing, shelter and entertainment.

Minerals

Minerals are typically solid, naturally occurring substances made up of atoms and ions that are arranged in regular three-dimensional patterns that give each mineral characteristic physical properties and chemical compositions.

Most minerals consist of chemical compounds – combinations of chemical elements – although some can appear as single elements, for example pure gold, silver and copper. Individual minerals have different characteristics such as:

- shape;

- the way that they break;

- taste;

- feel;

- magnetism.

Rocks

Rocks are aggregates of one of more minerals and are categorized according to how they are formed.

Igneous rocks (from the Latin word for 'fiery') are formed by the cooling and crystallization of molten rock-making material called magma or lava. Good examples of igneous rocks are granite and basalt. Hardening of these rocks may take place within the Earth's crust. Igneous rocks are particularly useful as building materials, because of their hardness and because they can be shaped into regular 'bricks' or 'blocks' with straight edges.

Sedimentary rocks are produced from the weathering and erosion of igneous rocks and other deposits of minerals. These range from huge boulders to materials that are carried in solution, for example in rain water.

Loose sediments can then be converted into solid sediments through pressure and by cementing processes due to chemical reaction. Sedimentary rocks tend to be deposited in layers.

Sandstone and shale that have formed from gravel, sand, mud and clay are typical sedimentary rocks. Limestone is another form of sedimentary rock that is formed from the deposit of animal shells over a long period of time. Again these materials are useful for building but are not as hard wearing as igneous ones, but they can be more readily shaped.

Metamorphic rocks are those that have changed their form. They may have been igneous or sedimentary originally but have been transformed in the Earth's crust by heat, chemical action or pressure. Some metamorphic rocks appear in sheets – for example, slate which was extensively used for roofing. Marble is a recrystallized limestone.

Extracting metals

Some of the most important products of the Earth are the metals that we use:

- in buildings and constructions such as bridges – for example, iron girders;

- in cars, aeroplanes, trains and other vehicles;

- in telecommunications – for example, in telegraphic wiring and internet connections;

- in all sorts of household appliances such as cookers and washing machines;

- in leisure activities – for example, in gym equipment and bicycles.

We use the term *metal ore* to describe a mineral that contains enough metal to make it worthwhile to extract the metal. Extracting a metal from its ore involves creating a chemical reaction to separate the metal. Metal can be extracted by:

- electrolysis – breaking the metal down by passing an electric current through it; or

- chemical reduction using carbon or carbon monoxide to obtain the iron.

The more reactive a metal is the harder it is to extract it, and the more reactive metals tend to be extracted using electrolysis. Less reactive metals can be extracted by chemical reduction.

Some commonly used metals with technological applications are:

- Iron, which can be made into a stronger substance – steel – which is used in construction (for example building houses, flats, skyscrapers, bridges) and transport (cars, ships and trains). Stainless steel is a higher-quality steel that does not rust easily and is used, for example, in razor blades, knives and cooking pans, and on boats and ships.

- Aluminium is a much less dense material, making it lighter. It is easy to bend and shape. It is very strong and it does not corrode. It is also a good conductor of heat and electricity. It therefore finds uses in aeroplanes, bicycle frames, vehicle body panels, drink cans, window frames and ladders.

- Copper is a material that is easily bent, does not corrode and is a good conductor. You will therefore find it being used in gas and water pipes because they can be bent without fracturing. It is also used in electric wires because, again, they can be easily bent and it is a good conductor of electricity. Copper can be created into an alloy with other metals – for example forming bronze, which is often used in coins, and in musical instruments. It has an attractive finish and is therefore used in ornaments and expensive cooking pans.

Limestone

Another good example of a product that is a natural resource from the Earth is limestone, which is formed from sedimentary rocks that were originally deposited as seashells.

Limestone can easily be quarried into blocks, which can be used as a building material as witnessed by many of the world's famous ancient cathedrals. Because it is an easy material for stonemasons to work with, it is also used in sculpting statues. Limestone chippings are often also used in road building. One of the most widely used applications of limestone is in the creation of cement. Clay is roasted with limestone in a kiln to create the cement. Cement is then mixed with water and sand, and the chemical reaction creates a very hard material that is widely used in buildings in the form of concrete, which hardens as the water dries out.

A further application with which you will be familiar is glass, where limestone is heated up with sand and soda to create a clear liquid substance that can then be shaped (often blown) to create a range of useful material such as windows, glasses and goblets.

Another use for limestone in a powdered form is to reduce the acidity that naturally occurs in many soils and also in lakes that have been contaminated by acid rain.

Questions

1 The name we give to Earth science is:

a astronomy;

b chemistry;

c geology;

d zoology.

2 The specific gravity of Earth taken as a whole is:

a the same as for the Earth's oceans;

b higher in the crust of the Earth than at the Earth's core;

c uniform throughout the layers of the Earth;

d lower in the rocks at the Earth's surface than in the Earth's core.

3 The hydrosphere:

a is the envelope of gases surrounding the Earth;

b is partially made up of water;

   c submerges about 71 per cent of the Earth's surface;

   d is mainly found in desert zones.

4 Movements in the Earth's mantle:

   a reduce the specific density of the Earth's core;

   b can lead to continental drift;

   c are contained entirely within the mantle;

   d are principally triggered by ocean tides.

5 Which of the following comprises the bulk of the volume of the Earth:

   a the oceans;

   b the outer core;

   c the mantle;

   d the crust?

6 The most common element in the outer 10 miles of the Earth's surface is:

   a magnesium;

   b iron;

   c silicon;

   d oxygen.

7 Which of the following is an example of an igneous rock:

   a sandstone;

   b shale;

   c limestone;

   d basalt?

8 Which of the following is an example of a sedimentary rock:

   a sandstone;

   b basalt;

   c granite;

   d marble?

9 Which of the following is an example of a metamorphic rock?

   a sandstone;

   b basalt;

c marble;

d shale?

10 Iron and steel are most likely to be produced by:

a electrolysis;

b magnetism;

c chemical reduction;

d sedimentation.

11 The bodies of aeroplanes are most likely to be made from:

a iron;

b steel;

c copper;

d aluminium.

12 Razor blades are most likely to be made from:

a brass;

b copper;

c stainless steel;

d aluminium.

13 Electrical wiring is most likely to be made out of:

a iron;

b stainless steel;

c copper;

d aluminium.

14 Limestone is an example of a:

a sedimentary rock;

b igneous rock;

c metamorphic rock;

d alloy.

15 Which of the following is not a common application of limestone:

a building blocks;

b cement;

c statues;

d girders?

16 Glass is made by combining and heating:

a Sand, soda and limestone;

b Clay and limestone;

c Iron, soda and limestone;

d Sand, aluminium and limestone.

key terms

energy

The capacity to do work.

radiation

The emission of energy as electromagnetic waves or as moving particles.

kinetic energy

The energy of motion of a mass.

work

The work done by any force is the product of the force and the distance moved in the direction of the force. If the force is exactly along the direction of motion, then the work done is just:
work = force × distance moved. ▶

■ Key natural forces and sources and forms of energy

Everything in the universe falls into one of two categories – energy or matter. The energy in the universe consists of radiation. In the definitions set out above we have said that energy is the capacity to do work – for example, to move a motor vehicle along, to heat a pan of soup, or to fuel a central-heating system.

Most of the Earth's energy comes from the sun but as yet we make very little use of solar power. However, other forms of energy also come from the sun. For example, prehistoric plants stored the sun's energy in their leaves. When they died they eventually formed coal seams, which store the energy until it is burnt as a coal – a form of fossil fuel.

The same logic can be applied to wind and wave power. Waves are formed by the winds, and winds blow because the sun warms our atmosphere. Warm air tends to rise, causing other air to move in to replace it.

Most of the mass-production power stations that we see around the country burn coal, oil or natural gas to run their generators. Others use uranium or the flow of water. Electricity is then transmitted around the country along high-voltage power lines.

Trophic levels

One of the unfortunate things about energy is that human consumers only receive a small percentage of energy that is created from the sun, although scientists are busy trying to use solar power more effectively. We cannot use the sun's energy directly for food. In contrast, plants use

geothermal energy

Energy from the internal heat of the Earth.

distillation

This is the purifying of a liquid by vaporizing and then condensing it and collecting the resulting liquid.

energy from the sun to grow roots, pump water and perform other functions.

Plants (termed producers) capture energy and they are able to pass on this energy as food to their consumers. However, they can only pass on about 10 per cent of the energy they receive as food.

Animals that eat the plants are termed primary consumers and they use this food energy to keep themselves warm and to perform bodily functions. The food that they do not use is excreted as waste.

If we eat a rabbit we only receive about 10 per cent of its energy – in this case we are secondary consumers.

If we ate a tuna fish that had fed on small fish which in turn had fed on plants we would be tertiary consumers.

Food consumption therefore follows a pyramid-shaped pattern in which available energy becomes lower at each stage. This is called the trophic pyramid (the word trophic refers to nutrition).

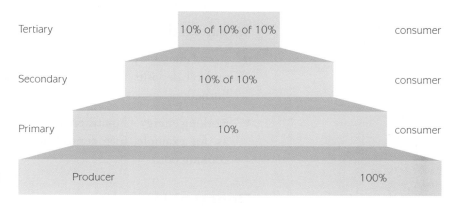

The trophic pyramid

Tertiary	10% of 10% of 10%	consumer
Secondary	10% of 10%	consumer
Primary	10%	consumer
Producer		100%

Different forms of energy

Energy comes in a number of forms:

- *Heat – thermal energy.* Thermal energy is energy that exists within a body due to the motion of the atoms that make up that body. Thermal energy is found within hot springs where water comes into contact with the hot rock making up the basement of a continent. Volcanoes also erupt as a result of thermal energy.

- *Light – radiant energy.* This is the energy carried by light. It is this energy that makes the photosynthesis process possible in the growth of plants.

- *Mechanical energy.* This is the kind of energy used by machines. For example, levers, gears and wheels can use mechanical energy to carry out work. Other forms of mechanical energy include landslides, avalanches and rain. To make rain, the sun evaporates water, which condenses into clouds. This water then falls as rain – rather like a great big machine.

- *Electrical energy.* This is energy that is stored in the back-and-forth motion of electrons in electric cables. Lightning involves the transformation of electrical energy into thermal energy and light energy.

- *Chemical energy.* This comes from chemical reactions. This is energy that has been stored in chemical form, such as in fuels or sugars or as energy stored in car batteries. Petrol is a chemical that combines with oxygen and a little thermal energy to release the thermal energy stored in the chemical structure of petrol.

- *Nuclear energy.* This comes from nuclear reaction. Nuclear energy becomes available when unstable nuclei spontaneously change by throwing off particles. The decay of the neutron into a proton, an electron and an antineutrino is an illustration of the conversion of nuclear mass energy into kinetic energy.

We can also classify energy according to whether it is:

- stored energy – potential energy as, for example, energy stored in coal and oil deposits that are waiting to be mined or drilled and then burned; or

- working energy – kinetic energy, which is energy that is being released as, for example, in a central-heating system or the flame under a cooking pot.

Renewable and non-renewable energy

Renewable energy

Renewable energy is a source that we can use over and over again, whereas non-renewable energy is an energy source that we are using up and cannot recreate in the short period of time – for example, because oil is made from the crushed bodies of creatures that died millions of years ago it is considered non-renewable.

Examples of renewable energy are:

- solar energy, from the sun;

- wind and geothermal energy from inside the Earth;

- biomass from plants;

- hydropower from water.

Renewable energy is an important source of energy, particularly in the generation of electricity. However, the sad fact is that in 2000 the overall use of renewable fuels had declined by almost 9 per cent from its 1996 peak.

The use of renewable energy is not new. In the middle of the nineteenth century, wood supplied up to 90 per cent of our energy needs. However, because of the low price and convenience of fossil fuels the use of wood has fallen. Nevertheless, biomass from manufacturing waste, black liquor from paper production, and rice hulls are being converted into electricity in some parts of the world.

One of the major problems for renewable fuels is that their supplies are not guaranteed on a regular pattern – for example there is no wind energy on a still day, cloudy days produce little solar power, and the energy of wave movements is very difficult to harness because the sea can be so violent.

Non-renewable

Most of our energy comes from non-renewable energy sources, which include the fossil fuels – oil, natural gas and coal. They are called fossil fuels because they were formed over millions of years by the action of heat from the Earth's core and pressure from rock and soil on the remains (or 'fossils') of dead plants and animals. Another non-renewable energy source is the element uranium, whose atoms can be split (through a process called nuclear fission) to create heat and ultimately electricity.

We use all these energy sources to generate the electricity we need for our homes, businesses, schools and factories. Electricity 'energizes' our computers, lights, refrigerators and washing machines, to name only a few of its uses.

analyse
this

example of a fossil fuel – petroleum (oil)

Oil was formed from the remains of animals and plants that lived millions of years ago in a marine environment before the dinosaurs. Over the years, layers of mud covered the remains. Heat and pressure from these layers helped the remains turn into what we today call crude oil. The word 'petroleum' means 'rock oil' or 'oil from the Earth'.

Crude oil is a smelly, yellow-to-black liquid and is usually found in underground areas called reservoirs. Scientists and technologists examine pictures taken of the underground site and, if it is promising, will excavate it. Above the hole, a structure called a 'derrick' is built to house the tools and pipes that go into the well to bring out the oil.

The crude oil is then transported to a refinery, which is the oil company's 'factory' where the crude oil is turned into the products that people want – fuels, greases, waxes, bitumen, base oils for lubricants, and chemical feedstocks for use by companies manufacturing paint, detergents, pharmaceuticals and plastics.

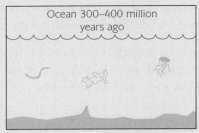

Sea plants and animals died and were buried on the ocean floor, where they were covered by layers of sand and silt.

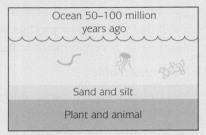

Over millions of years remains were buried deeper and deeper. Heat and pressure turned them into oil and gas.

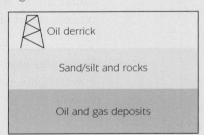

Today we can drill down through the sand/silt and rock to bring out the oil.

The formation of petroleum and natural gas

The basic aim is to turn the crude oil into the most valuable products as efficiently as possible and with minimum waste.

The refinery must convert more of each barrel of crude oil into the lighter 'whiter' oil products for which the market is prepared to pay more – such as petrol and aviation fuel – rather than the 'black' products, such as fuel oils.

Sophisticated procedures have been evolved to achieve this. For instance, the price and quality of available crudes can be fed into a computer system, which already 'knows' all the manufacturing and distribution options. The system then 'recommends' the refinery that can best make specific products in particular quantities and using particular methods.

The 'recommendations' can be affected by such unforeseeable problems as fog at sea – which may prevent the tanker reaching the refinery as expected.

The main refinery processes

The crude oil is first passed through one or more physical separation processes ('physical' because they do not create chemical changes – no new compounds are formed). The main physical technique is distillation. The distilling units at refineries can accept many different kinds of crude, the precise one chosen at any time is dependent on a complex equation of supply, demand and cost.

Partly refined products can then be passed through chemical conversion processes that produce a change in the size and structure of the hydrocarbon molecules – in other words, they create new products, the 'added value' products on which the success of the whole operation depends.

The basic chemical conversion processes, each of them capable of many variations, include 'cracking', in which the heavier components are converted into lighter 'added value' products such as petrol. One of the latest and most effective cracking processes is 'hyrdrocracking', which can split the heavy feedstocks into a particularly wide range of products.

Another important chemical conversion process is 'platforming', which can produce high-octane blending components for low lead or unleaded petrol.

The financial success of the refinery depends on turning the crude oil into as many expensive products as possible while keeping costs as low as possible.

Questions

1 Why is petroleum oil considered to be a non-renewable source of energy?

2 Give five examples of uses that crude oil can be put to after it has been refined.

3 Describe one physical and one chemical process that is carried out in a refinery.

4 How dependent are you and your family on products that are based on crude oil?

5 Is this a good or bad thing?

Here are some multiple-choice questions.

1 Which of the following is the best example of a renewable source of energy:

a oil;

b natural gas;

c biomass;

d petroleum?

2 Which of the following is the best example of a non-renewable source of energy:

a nuclear;

b wave;

c wind;

d biomass?

3 What is the term used to refer to energy derived directly from the sun:

a geothermal;

b biomass;

c solar;

d fossil?

4 What percentage of their energy do plants pass on to their consumers in food energy:

a 100 per cent;

b 10 per cent;

c 1 per cent;

d nothing?

5 Which of the following would receive or generate the most energy in the trophic pyramid:

a producers;

b primary consumers;

c secondary consumers;

d tertiary consumers?

6 What do we call the type of energy that we would find in a hot-water geyser:

a thermal;

b radiant;

c mechanical;

d chemical?

7 Light energy used by plants in the photosynthesis process is referred to as:

a mechanical;

b nuclear;

c radiant;

d electrical.

8 When petrol combines with oxygen to give energy, the main form of energy being generated is:

a nuclear;

b thermal;

c stored;

d chemical.

9 Which of the following is the best example of working energy as opposed to stored energy:

a oil deposits under the oceans;

b coal in a coal bunker;

c gas in a gas cylinder;

d electricity cooking a pot of stew?

10 The main source of hydropower is:

a wind;

b waves;

c nuclear reaction;

d biomass.

11 Which of the following is not a fossil fuel:

a uranium;

b coal;

c natural gas;

d oil?

12 An oil company's factory is termed its:

a derrick;

b geyser;

    c refinery;

    d field.

13 The main physical process in separating crude oil is that of:

    a cracking;

    b distillation;

    c drilling;

    d platforming.

14 Adding value to oil based products can be done by all of the following except:

    a changing the size and structure of the hydrocarbon molecules;

    b concentrating on producing low-grade products;

    c converting heavier products into lighter products such as petrol;

    d platforming to produce high-octane blending components.

After reading this chapter and answering the questions, consider the following issues.

1 How do you think the universe first came into being? Do you think that scientific explanations can provide all the answers?

2 Is Earth a particularly special place, or is it just 'one place to be' in the universe?

3 What are the main sources of energy that we use? Are they renewable or non-renewable? Is there a danger of burning up too many non-renewable energy sources?

4 How bountiful is our planet? What are the key resources that our planet provides for us?

6

The nature of life

Earth does not occupy a special place in the heavens. It is not the 'centre of the universe'. In fact it is quite an ordinary planet, which is one of nine planets orbiting an unremarkable star. However, we do not yet know whether life exists elsewhere. So at the moment we are remarkable and we need to understand the reasons why life exists on our 'unique' life-carrying planet.

We have no evidence of life on other planets – yet! We do not know why life exists on Earth, and we do not know where else life exists apart from Earth. Many scientists believe that it is highly likely that life exists elsewhere, but they do not know what form that life takes – whether it is simply living microbial matter on other planets, or whether advanced civilizations exist in parts of the universe that are similar to our own.

analyse this

Here are some questions for discussion.

1 Why does life exist on our planet?

2 Is there likely to be life elsewhere?

3 What properties does something need to have for it to be living?

4 What sorts of conditions would need to exist on other planets for them to contain life forms?

Apollo astronauts have said that the Earth, with its blue water and white clouds, was by far the most inviting object they could see in the sky when they were on the moon. Their bias is understandable. They knew from intimate observations what this planet is like and could translate the sight of clouds, oceans and continents into everyday experiences of, say, a sea breeze blowing surf onto a sunny beach.

One cannot be sure of the range of chemical environments that will support life. All that is known now is that the Earth supports life and that its life depends on the continuous existence of liquid water. At present the Earth is the only planet known to satisfy that condition. Earth's continuous record of life for at least the past five billion years shows that liquid water has been available during all that time.

Life on Earth is based on the unique properties of the carbon atom, although it is possible that there are other forms of biochemistry. Carbon is the most versatile of all the elements because its atoms are able to form chemical bonds that create especially long and complex molecules.

■ The atomic structure of life

Living things are made up of atoms. However, these atoms are similar to those atoms that make up non-living things. Take, for example, oxygen, which is the most common component of living things – but it also appears in air, the rivers and seas, and the rocks as well.

Is there any difference between the organic molecules that make up living things and the inorganic molecules that make up non-living things?

Organic molecules are usually larger, they are made up of thousands of atoms. Non-organic molecules typically consist of fewer than a dozen atoms.

Another important difference is that living things only consist of 24 different atoms, whereas inorganic molecules can be made up of any of the

The 24 atoms that make up life

Atom	% of human body by weight
Hydrogen	9.5
Carbon	18.5
Nitrogen	3.3
Oxygen	6.5
Fluorine	trace
Sodium	0.2
Magnesium	0.1
Silicon	trace
Phosphorous	1.0
Sulphur	0.3
Chlorine	0.2
Potassium	0.4
Calcium	1.5
Vanadium	trace
Chromium	trace
Manganese	trace
Iron	trace
Cobalt	trace
Copper	trace
Zinc	trace
Selenium	trace
Molybdenum	trace
Tin	trace
Iodine	trace

92 kinds of atoms that are found on Earth. In fact, 99 per cent of all organic molecules consists of just six atoms: carbon, hydrogen, nitrogen, oxygen, phosphorous and sulphur. These are atoms that exist close to the surface of the Earth's crust.

The atoms that life is made up of tend to be relatively small. These smaller atoms are much better at binding together than are larger atoms.

■ The genetic structure of life

The difference between humans and other forms of life lies in differences in cell types and structures. Whereas an amoeba only has one cell, which does not do much except seek out food, take it in, use it and then grow and multiply, humans are made up of about 10 trillion cells, consisting of many different types, many of which specialize in different types of things.

Our cells are made up of atoms or molecules (atoms chemically bonded together).

Our cells are dived into two parts, the 'nucleus' and the 'cytoplasm' separated by a nuclear membrane. Inside the nucleus we find our 'genes'. Genes determine the structure and activities of living things. They also help to pass a set of characteristics on to the next generation of cells. Genes are therefore the agents of heredity and are what help to give us the characteristics of our parents.

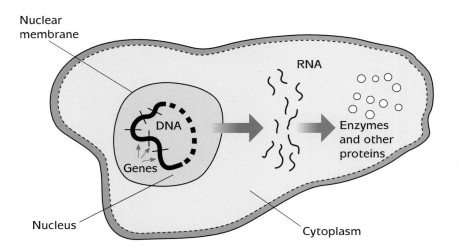

Genes are distinct regions of very long, thin molecules of the chemical deoxyribonucleic acid (DNA). Human cells contain bundles of DNA, each known as a 'chromosome'. The DNA of each chromosome contains many genes. Our genes carry the 'information' (in a chemically coded form) needed to make an organism, and they pass that information on to following generations of cells.

In Chapter 4 we saw that the genes are the result of the combination of four nucleotides into a series of three-letter sequences, and that each gene is a 'sentence' composed of words in a specific order. Each gene has a specific function – which, in the case of humans, helps us to be human – to grow bigger, to communicate with each other, to reproduce, to move around and, of course, to think intelligent thoughts.

■ The evolution of life forms

Andrew Scott, in a book entitled *The Creation of Life*, sets out to define what he means by 'life' in the following way:

All the creatures that everyone accepts to be alive without question, such as ourselves, and cats and fleas and so on, are believed to have developed from simpler creatures by evolution. The ability to evolve by natural selection is what has allowed simple things to give rise to more complex things like ourselves. So if we can identify the point in life's history at which evolution began, and if we can divide everything around us into those that can evolve and those that cannot, then I think we will have marked the dividing line between the dead and the alive as best we can (although still somewhat ambiguously, since there can be arguments about what counts as true evolution).

What are the requirements for any thing to be able to 'evolve'? The first point to make is that individual things never evolve, in the biological sense of the word – it is populations that evolve. Each individual human, or ape or cat, or other living thing, stays the same creature throughout its life, but they are all part of evolving populations, since the structure of the individuals of the populations changes over many generations.

Some people use the term 'evolution' simply to describe any changes over a period of time, but that is not the sense in which it is being used here. I am using it in the strict biological sense of 'change in a population through the generations, powered by the continuous selection of favourable characteristics'. I purposely avoided using the term 'natural' selection in that definition, because we ourselves make some species evolve by 'artificial' selection. When we select dogs with particularly floppy ears, or horses that run faster than others, or flowers with the heaviest scents, and use them for further breeding, we are artificially selecting characteristics that would not necessarily be selected in nature. This artificial selection can still make hounds and horses and flowers evolve – in fact they evolve much more quickly than they would normally, because we, God-like, reach down and do the selecting; and they evolve in directions often different to the ones that natural selection would have taken.

So to define 'life' we are looking for the requirements for evolution, and in fact we have already met them. The members of any population that is to evolve by natural or artificial selection must be replicated from time to time; during the course of that replication changes must sometimes occur that make the replicas slightly different from the originals; and these changes must be able to affect the speed and efficiency with which the individuals become replicated. Anything that has these properties will be able to give rise to a population of things that evolves by selection. How far that evolution will take the population towards thing we would clearly accept as alive, depends on how much scope there is for variant things to alter and organise their environment in ways that favour their own replication. But populations of things that can evolve clearly have the potential to give rise to things we would all accept as 'alive'. That is why, if we are to decide on a dividing line between the dead and the living, then the threshold of evolution seems to be the place to draw it.

Questions

1 Do you agree with the definition of life given by Andrew Scott in the discussion above? Explain why you agree or disagree.

2 Using Andrew Scott's definition, can you identify things that are living and those things that are not living? Does his definition hold up?

3 Using his definition, at what point might life start to develop on other planets, or new life forms start to develop on our own planet?

■ The development of life forms with which we are familiar

Life as we know it has developed over millions of years. Your lifetime may seem to be incredibly long but it can be seen as just the blink of an eye taken against the history of life on this planet. Our planet has been active for 4.6 billion years, and it shows no sign of calming down. The Earth's atmosphere, oceans, thin crust and deep interior have been in motion since they were formed. Life has been an integral part of the surface for at least four-fifths of the planet's history.

Man is a relatively new arrival on the Earth, but in recent years has come to dominate the planet. It has not always been so. The dominant species will always be those that are best adapted to meet environmental conditions.

At one time the dinosaurs were masters of the Earth when it was full of lush green vegetation, then the reptiles followed in an age of darkness. Today it is mankind that dominates the Earth. Who will follow us?

You will be familiar with the age when the dinosaurs ruled the Earth. They were able to do so because of their size and their ability to live on the lush vegetation that was available to them. Contrary to Disney images of the dinosaurs, many were vegetarian rather than meat eaters.

However, the age of the dinosaurs came to an abrupt end; one theory suggests that this occurred when a giant comet struck the Earth. The impact of this collision created a giant tidal wave coupled with a massive cloud of rock and dust that covered the Earth, turning everything very cold and freezing up the surface of the planet. The sun would have been obscured for a long period of time.

It was the reptiles who were able to benefit from this situation including alligators, crocodiles and dragon lizards. They were cold blooded and so were able to hibernate in the frozen conditions. Eventually, when the sun began to emerge, they were able to live on the carcasses of rotting animals such as dinosaurs. Reptiles are able to live on rotten meat and so were able to dominate the planet for a considerable period until other life forms, such as the apes and eventually man, were able to carve out their own niches.

■ Would it be possible to create life?

Today, many scientists believe that it is not too difficult to create life forms given the right sorts of ingredients. Charles Pellegrino explains how this could be done in a book called *Darwin's Universe*:

Life from nonlife. You could start the process in your own kitchen, if you wanted to. It's that easy. Assemble carbon, hydrogen, nitrogen, and oxygen in one place (methane and ammonia gas over water will do nicely), apply heat, shock waves, X-rays, or ultraviolet radiation – almost any form of energy input – and, invariably, within 20 hours or so, you will have incited the formation of carbon compounds ranging from simple amino acids to complex organic microstructures resembling spheroids, rods, and hollow tubes with tantalizing septalike divisions. Yet such experiments involve only small volumes over very short periods of time. What could be done with entire oceans over a period of millions, or billions, of years? You need only look out of your window or into a mirror to see.

■ Is there life elsewhere?

In recent years a string of new planets has been found beyond our own solar system, revealed by the fact that their gravitational influence causes nearby stars to wobble. Over 30 planets have been detected in this way, including one seen in silhouette, floating past its own sun.

One of Jupiter's moons, Europa, is likely to be covered by an iced-over ocean – could life exist in this ocean?

In December 1999 scientists announced that they had detected the first reflected light from a distant planet, which raises the prospect of analysing the chemical composition of the planet to search for signs of life. The latest batch of exoplanets even contains worlds that orbit in the habitable zone of their parent stars, where liquid water and life could exist.

A number of scientists believe that humankind's recent appearance on Earth was dependent on an unlikely chain of events – a large moon, plate tectonics, a salubrious atmosphere, a placid sun, and even the presence of large planetary neighbours such as Jupiter and Saturn. The argument is that the probability of all these conditions existing at the same time is highly unlikely (but it has been known for the same person to win the lottery more than once). The scientist Seth Shostak argues that one should be wary of probabilities calculated after the fact. He goes on to argue that in searching for signs of life 'out there' we should sail the sea of discovery. He quotes Giuseppi Cocconi and Philip Morrison who in the 1960s argued that 'the probability of success is difficult to estimate, but if we never search, the chance of success is zero.'

Planet watchers are becoming increasingly excited about the prospect of discovering new worlds beyond our own. Scientists have found that various forms of life continue to exist on Earth in the most hostile conditions. For example, microbial life exists in the most bleak and threatening polar conditions. If life can exist in the most hostile places on Earth then there is potential for it to exist on other planets.

In recent times interest has increasingly focused on the moons of Jupiter, which may potentially contain life.

Perhaps the most important contribution that Galileo made to science was the discovery, on 7 January 1610, of the four moons around Jupiter, which are today called Io, Europa, Gannymede and Callisto.

Scientists have recently focused their attention on Io and Europa. The amazing thing about Io is that it experiences volcanic eruptions and spews into the air volcanic ash, which rises a great distance from the surface of this moon before falling back again. The ash rises much higher than on Earth because of the low gravitational pull of the planet.

Europa is even more exciting because it is believed to be covered by an icy substance, which might contain a liquid water ocean under the ice. Researchers from the University of Arizona believe that curved cracks on the surface of this ice covering are caused by tidal stresses from the subsurface of the ocean.

The varying distances of Europa from Jupiter are believed to cause tides in the ocean to rise and fall as the distance between Europa and Jupiter fluctuates. Voyager mapped part of the surface of Europa in 1979.

Another explanation for the cracks in the surface of Europa is that they are caused by a series of volcanic eruptions or geysers. If this is the case then there is a strong potential for there to be life under the surface of the ocean.

On Earth, life is rarely found at the bottom of our deepest oceans because they are so cold and hostile to life. However, probes have discovered life in our deepest oceans where there is volcanic activity that provides heat and life. Fish and other sea creatures are abundant in these areas of volcanic activity. NASA is planning a Europa orbiter mission. This would include instruments such as an ice-penetrating radar that could see through the ice to any ocean below.

A number of scientists believe that there may well be life out there, but we have not yet started looking for it properly. The starting point is to discover microbial matter, which may exist in the most hostile conditions. Of course, there is then a giant step forward to assuming that there is intelligent life. However, if we can accept the potential of there being 'life' out there, it may help us to understand that we might not be as unique as we think we are. Of course, this should not hurt too much. After all, it was Galileo who showed that the sun did not revolve around the Earth – and we have been able to adjust to this realization.

Currently, the USA's 'Search for Extraterrestrial Intelligence' (SETI) programme is beaming out regular signals to distant galaxies to seek for signs of a response, to seek extraterrestrial life. These signals are very simple. Of course, if they are ever received, the return signal will be from beings that do not exist in the same period of time as us.

analyse
this

Here are some questions for discussion.

1   If there is life on other planets would you expect it to consist of the same atoms and molecules as life on Earth?

2   What sort of genetic structure would you expect life on other planets to have?

3   What conditions would you expect to exist on other planets for life to exist there?

4   Do you believe that there is life on other planets? Why?

5   What would be the dangers of meeting up with new life forms with which we are not familiar?

Organic molecules like those that have created life on Earth are widely scattered throughout our galaxy. Giant molecular clouds in interstellar space contain a substantial amount of carbon atoms that have combined with oxygen atoms to make the simple carbon monoxide molecule. But carbon atoms have also combined with other elements to produce many organic compounds.

Since the 1960s radio astronomers have detected tell-tale microwave emission lines from interstellar clouds that help identify dozens of these carbon-based chemicals. There is additional evidence of extraterrestrial organic molecules from newly fallen meteorites, which often contain a variety of organic substances.

Given the current state of technology on Earth it would be impossible to create a spacecraft to visit other stars. It would take too long and be too expensive. Instead, scientists are working on seeking to pick up alien radio transmissions.

Since 1995 the independent SETI institute has been using advanced radio techniques to listen to transmissions from over 1000 solar-type stars – no confirmed, repeating signals have turned up.

Frank Drake, an American space researcher, has devised a simple equation to calculate the likelihood of life existing elsewhere in the galaxy. Don't worry too much about the mathematics of the equation, which reads:

$$N = R_*f_pn_cf_lf_if_cL$$

Where:

N = the number of technologically advanced civilizations in the galaxy whose messages we would be able to detect;

$R_* =$ the rate at which solar-type stars form in the galaxy;

$f_p =$ the fraction of stars that have planets;

$n_c =$ the number of planets per solar system that are Earthlike (suitable for life);

$f_l =$ the fraction of those Earthlike planets on which life actually arises;

$f_i =$ the fraction of those life forms that evolve into intelligent species;

$f_c =$ the fraction of those species that develop adequate technology and then choose to send messages out into space;

$L =$ the lifetime of that techologically advanced society.

By examining the various components of the equation it becomes clear that mathematically it may be possible to estimate the chance of there being life out there – for example we can obtain R^* and f_p by observation.

The problem is of course that if we detect a signal from a far distant planet then the civilization that sent it may no longer be in existence – life on Earth developed billions of years ago. Of course there may be planets that are capable of developing intelligent life where that life has not evolved as yet, in which case we will miss them.

The idea that there is life on other planets has required a shift in our thinking. At one time we thought we were the centre of the universe, and that everything revolved around mankind. Later we found that the Earth revolved around the sun, and then that there were many stars containing planetary systems. If there is life on other planets then we may be just one type of poorly developed planet whose development is insignificant when compared with the achievements of people living in other galaxies.

If there is life elsewhere in the universe we will have to radically change our thinking about the nature of existence and the importance of mankind in the order of things.

A wide range of values have been proposed for the terms in the Drake equation, producing a variety of different estimates of N. Some scientists agree that there is only one advanced civilization in the Galaxy, whereas others calculate that there may be hundreds or thousands of planets containing such civilizations.

Questions

1 Life as we know it is based on the versatility of one particular atom, which is:

a carbon;

b oxygen;

c hydrogen;

d lithium.

2 Living things are typically made up of each of the following except:

a organic molecules;

b thousands of atoms;

c 24 different atoms;

d a single atom.

3 The three most important atoms as a percentage of human body weight are:

a carbon, nitrogen and magnesium;

b oxygen, carbon and hydrogen;

c hydrogen, carbon and nitrogen;

d carbon, silicon, oxygen.

4 Humans are made up of:

a a single cell;

b about 10 trillion cells;

c interacting pairs of cells;

d non-cellular structures.

5 The structure and activities of living things, and hereditary characteristics in humans, are passed on by our:

a cytoplasm;

b genes;

c molecules;

d blood.

6 Human cells do not contain:

a genes;

b DNA;

c chromosomes;

d chlorophyl.

7 What species were best adapted to survive the period immediately after a giant comet hit the planet:

a dinosaurs;

b man;

c reptiles;

d birds?

8 Who was it that first observed Jupiter's moon:

a Newton;

b Kepler;

c Drake;

d Galileo?

9 Which of the moons of Jupiter is covered by an icy substance:

a Io;

b Gannymede;

c Callisto;

d Europa?

10 The Drake equation is designed to calculate:

a the number of other civilizations that exist in our galaxy;.

b the proportion of stars that have planets;

c the number of technologically advanced civilizations in the galaxy whose messages we would be able to detect;

d the proportion of those species that develop adequate technology and then choose to send messages out into space.

11 The number of planets with advanced forms of life is:

a one;

b between one and 100;

c between 100 and 1000;

d not known.

Here are some more general questions for you to consider.

1 What do you think is meant by life?

2 Is there more to life than chemical and biological existence?

3 Is it a good or bad thing that life might exist on other planets?

4 What sorts of conditions would you expect to find on other planets if life exists there?

5 Is the Earth the best place on which to be alive?

7

Science, technology and human progress

Celebrity Fit Club members –
obesity is one of the spin-offs of
the modern diet and lifestyle

We live in a society in which science and technology have helped to provide more plentiful supplies of food for us than ever before and in which
there is an increasing trend towards ready-cooked meals, take-away food
and convenience meals. Breakthroughs in food technology provide us
with a range of meals that can be instantly prepared and that are based
on detailed research into consumer preferences. Yet this is also a world of
increasing obesity, in which one in three school children is clinically
obese. Does this mean that breakthroughs in the science and technology
of food cultivation and preparation provide us with better lives? Are we
living in an age of progress?

Questions

1 Do scientists and technologists have a responsibility to provide us with healthier food?

2 Whose responsibility is it that many people live unhealthy life styles?

3 Is obesity an inevitable downside of progress?

The concept of human progress is slippery because what one person refers to as progress may not be so to another person. For example, some people like to put double glazing into their houses and fill them with all the latest gadgets – a hob, air extractor, en suite bathroom, wide-screen television and so on – whereas other people prefer to keep their houses simple and detest modern-day gadgets.

Science and technology are seen by many as the means by which progress is achieved because scientific discovery and technological innovation have led to the creation of all the artefacts and systems that make our lives more comfortable:

key terms

cosmology

Science of the origin and development of the universe.

autism

Mental condition characterized by complete self-absorption and a reduced ability to respond to the outside world.

mimeograph

A duplicating machine that produces copies from a stencil.

science

The systematic study of nature and the behaviour of the material and physical universe, based on observation, experiment and measurement.

technology

The application of practical or mechanical sciences to industry or commerce.

antedated

Preceded.

- our understanding of the generation of energy, and heating systems, has made modern central heating possible;

- our understanding of the nature and properties of hydrocarbons has made it possible for us to get around by car of aeroplane, and so forth.

Scientific progress and technological innovation make it possible for us to exploit more of the natural resources of the planet and to use these resources for more and more applications. However, there are many people who would criticize this as a western perspective of progress – for example Mahatma Gandhi argued that we could live in an alternative way simply by using traditional local resources to meet local needs. Gandhi once said that 'If the rest of the world continues to develop by using resources in the same way as is done by that small island the United Kingdom, then we will strip the Earth bare like locusts.'

So what do you think is meant by progress, and what is the role of science and technology in this process? Read through the following two case studies and discuss the answers to the questions that follow.

analyse
this

is this progress?

How science helps us to live better lives – hunt narrows in the search for autism gene

By Nicholas Pyke, *Independent on Sunday,* 21 July 2002.

The worldwide search for the causes of autism is close to a decisive breakthrough, according to the British doctor at the forefront of the international investigation.

Dr Anthony Bailey, recently appointed the country's first professor of autism at Oxford University, believes that the first of the genes responsible for the condition could be identified within two years. The development raises the prospect of an effective medical treatment for a disorder that leaves children trapped in a world of their own, struggling to relate to others.

Autism has become increasingly common, affecting one child in every 200 according to some estimates. The condition is now emerging as a major concern for schools and medical services.

It has been at the centre of a long-running political controversy amid claims that there may be evidence linking the single measles/mumps/rubella vaccine for infants (MMR) with the condition. The result has been a drop in levels of childhood immunization, while the medical authorities refuse to offer the three vaccines separately. The problem here has been that of fairness, because a number of middle class parents have been able to afford to pay to have their children given the separate treatments, whereas poorer families worried about the effect of the MMR inoculation can not make this choice, or worse still may not have their children inoculated at all, leading to increased threats of an epidemic occurring.

Although identifying the genes behind autism is not the same as discovering a cure, which may still be many years away, Dr Bailey describes it as the crucial step in understanding and conquering the disorder. 'In terms of working out what's going wrong in the brain it's the key advance', he said. 'If we can identify these genes we can work out what the proteins are that these genes code for.'

'The first gene should be identified within the next two years. There's a fair amount of agreement about where to look.' Autism, like heart disease appears to be caused by a combination of factors, some of which may not be genetic. This makes the causes harder to track than in conditions such as cystic fibrosis or sickle cell anaemia.

But the breakthrough, when it comes, will revolutionise the hunt for treatments, allowing researchers to focus more accurately and work more quickly. It may also help doctors assess the chances of autism occurring in individual families.'

Questions

1 Why is autism an important concern for scientific investigation?

2 What is the significance of this breakthrough?

3 Why is the breakthrough only the first part of the story?

4 How might scientists and technologists be able to take the breakthrough further?

5 How does this example illustrate the role of science in making people's lives better?

6 In your view is it fair that the government is refusing to pay for single inoculations for measles, mumps and rubella? How might the breakthrough outlined in the article help this situation?

analyse
this

is this progress?

Self-focusing glasses

How science and technology help us to live better lives – Oxford professor invents self-focusing glasses

By Meg Kociemba and Jonathan Thompson, *Independent on Sunday,* 15 December 2002.

An Oxford physics professor is selling 10 million pairs of revolutionary new spectacles to Africa which enable the users to wear them for a lifetime without ever going to an optician.

The glasses could help the billion people around the world who are deprived of spectacles but suffer from long or near sight. Joshua Silver's simple invention could in theory help to eradicate adult illiteracy in developing countries.

Professor Silver's 'adaptive glasses' look like ordinary ones except for the two knobs on either side of the frame that can adjust the curvature of the lens. It means that in countries where opticians are scarce, wearers can simply alter the focus as their eyesight deteriorates over time.

Uncorrected poor vision is considered among the most serious problems in the developing world, holding back economies by forcing educated classes to retire early with failing eyesight.

The World Health Organisation (WHO) estimates one billion people worldwide need but do not have access to spectacles.

The lenses are filled with silicon oil, controlled via a small pump on the frame. This alters the curvature of the lens, allowing the wearer to see clearly with the simple turn of a knob. Through a deal with the WHO and the World Bank, Prof Silver plans to sell up to 400,000 adaptive glasses in Ghana with another deal for 9.3 million pairs in South Africa also in the pipeline. The glasses are sold at about £6 through his company Adaptive Eyecare, based in Oxford but cost less than that to make. With just 50 opticians in Ghana out of a population of almost 20 million, glasses that last a lifetime will prove a boon.

'It would take on average about 200 years to be seen by an optometrist in Ghana', explained Professor Silver, 'But adaptive glasses obviate the need for a trip at all.'

The Professor began work on his invention 17 years ago – although the technique of using liquid in lenses dates back to the 18th century.

Questions

1 Does the combination of science and technology involved in the self-focusing glasses provide an example of progress?

2 If so, what criteria do you feel are appropriate in deciding whether science and technology support progress?

3 Can you provide examples of where scientific and technological developments may not be considered as adding to progress?

■ Are science and technology neutral?

It is possible to argue that if science simply limits itself to the descriptive study of the laws of nature, then it has no moral or ethical quality and thus is neutral. It is often said that science simply seeks to find out the truth about nature. By forming and testing hypotheses it is possible to set out accurate descriptions of natural laws that can be seen as universal truths. Neutrality associated with scientific aims implies that neither good nor evil is intended from the results of scientific investigation; the aim is the pursuit of knowledge in itself.

Galileo stated that 'the conclusions of natural science are true and necessary, and the judgement of man has nothing to do with them.'

A number of eminent modern-day scientists have argued that the power of science enables us to better understand nature so that we no longer have to resort to superstition and magical explanations.

Richard Dawkins, in his famous book *The Selfish Gene*, claims that because we now have modern biology 'we no longer have to resort to superstition when faced with the deep problems'. This view is supported by Stephen Hawking in *A Brief History of Time*, who is a keen supporter of the wisdom of science, stating that:

Ever since the dawn of civilisation, people . . . have craved an understanding of the underlying order of the world. Today we still yearn to know why we are here and where we came from. Humanity's deepest desire for knowledge is justification enough for our continuing quest. And our goal is nothing less than a complete description of the universe we live in.

He writes that when a satisfactory cosmological theory has emerged:

we shall all – philosophers, scientists, and just ordinary people – be able to take part in the discussion of the question why it is that we and the universe exist. If we find the answer to that, it would be the ultimate triumph of human reason – for then we would know the mind of God.

However, there are others who question the neutrality of science. For example, they point to the way in which much scientific research is financed by giant companies like Shell, Nestlé and the chemical and pharmaceutical companies. They argue that because these corporations influence what is studied, this reduces some of the neutrality of scientific endeavour. Moreover, a number of companies may pay scientists large sums of money to produce opinions about healthy eating, or the impact of smoking, and so forth. Once you start paying large sums of money to the scientists that you employ you begin to reduce the neutrality of science. If you then consider that the work of scientists, including their published findings, is used to determine what is produced in society, you see that non-neutral science has the ability to influence 'progress' and shape the nature of the society that we live in.

Another challenge to 'neutrality' is associated with the deliberate suppression of scientific knowledge or the active promotion of particular theories that conform with a specific political situation. For example, it has been claimed that the UK government has suppressed some scientific research about the relationship between BSE in cattle and human forms of the disease while promoting other pieces of research that support its own view.

A difficult issue for scientists is the extent to which their work is wrapped up in what is seen as a purely scientific investigation and the extent to which they take on board value judgements based on moral and ethical beliefs. Scientists have to decide for example:

- whether they should be involved in work that can be used for nuclear weapons testing;

- whether they should be involved in work that enables the creation of clones.

The easy answer is to say, 'I am just a scientist an objective researcher seeking to find out how the world works – what use is made of my work is beyond my control.' However, this approach seems to involve an abdication of moral responsibility.

C.H. Waddington, in his 1941 book *The Scientific Attitude*, noted that:

Responsible scientists looking at their colleagues, saw the obvious fact that most specialists were quite unfitted to play an important part in the evolution of general culture; but, far from acknowledging that this was a sign of science's failure, they accepted it almost with glee as an excuse which let them out of the necessity of thinking about wider issues.

He went on to argue that scientists cannot divorce themselves from moral responsibility.

Similarly, there is a popular view that technology, considered as a collection of machines, techniques and tools, is neutral in that it does not hold any political or social views. Taking this view then technology would be seen to be neither good nor evil.

However, the end to which technology is used may be harmful. Where a particular application, such as a space satellite, chosen for its beneficial results, produces harmful side effects, such as modern warfare, then the blame is usually placed on the poor control of the application of technology. Technology can also be assumed to be neutral in the sense that technological development continues apace irrespective of the power structure in a country – in other words, irrespective of who is in government.

However, as with science, this is not necessarily the case. Those with most money and influence are best placed to decide what funding and research efforts will go into the development of different types of technology. For example, one of the most sophisticated technologies in the world today is weapons technology, particularly in the USA. This military technology can be used to enforce the political and social influence of the USA in the wider world. At the same time, efforts to provide appropriate technologies for the developing world are given very low priority, and frequently large western companies have foisted inappropriate technologies on the developing world – for example in the sphere of infant feeding in Africa.

Large multinationals have promoted powdered milk alternatives as a solution for African women, with very poor results. Where instructions have not been effectively communicated many women have substituted breast milk for infant-feeding products, which are expensive to use and are often used poorly. Diluted powdered milk from dirty bottles and dirty teats is often substituted for breast milk. This leads to malnutrition and dietary disorders such as diarrhoea or vomiting. Typically children who are fed on bottled milk weigh less and are less robust than breast-fed children.

Critics of the neutral technology view argue that the nature of a society's technology at any given moment reflects and supports the dominant social class and its values.

■ Are we masters or slaves of technological progress?

Advocates of science and technology as the means to progress argue that very few people would want to return to a past characterized by:

- lower periods of life expectancy;

- higher levels of illiteracy;

- frequent illness and disease;

- more widespread poverty.

They argue that science and technology have helped to free us to enjoy more leisure time and a greater range of leisure activities, to have access to better medical care, have freed women from domestic drudgery, and many other improvements.

However, there are many critics who argue that rather than science and technology freeing us it has restricted us, as illustrated by the following article written by Stuart Chase in 1929, in his introduction to his book *Men and Machines:*

Certain philosophers hold that machinery is enslaving us. I am not a machine tender, but first and last I encounter a good many mechanisms in a day's march, particularly when that day is spent in a city so large and so complicated that it could never have been built by human muscle. Before analysing the extent of serfdom in others, it might be well to determine how far I am myself a slave.

The first thing that I hear in the morning is a machine – a patented alarm clock. It calls and I obey. But if I do not feel like obeying, I touch its back, and it relapses humbly into silence. Thus we bully each other, with the clock normally leading by a wide margin. (Once, however, I threw a clock out of the window, and it never bullied anyone again.)

I arise and go into the bathroom. Here I take up a second mechanism, and after inserting a piece of leather between its rollers, move it briskly up and down before proceeding to scrape my face with it. I turn various faucets and a mixing valve, and a nickel dial studded with little holes showers me with water. Depending on the season, I may snap on electric lights and an electric heater. Downstairs, if it chances to be either the first or the fifteenth day of the month, I take a can with a very long nose, and oil an electric motor which blows petroleum into my furnace, a motor which runs the washing machine, and a motor which operates my refrigeration engine. Meanwhile an electric range is cooking my breakfast, and on the table slices of bread are being heated by an electrical toaster which makes a buzzing sound in its vitals, and then suddenly splits open when the toast is browned to a turn. If time allow,

I may play a little tune on the piano which stands near the breakfast table, noting the delicate system of levers and hammers upon which the mechanisms is based. Before I leave the house, the whine of the vacuum cleaner is already in my ears.

I go to the garage, and by proper and sometimes prolonged manipulations, start explosions in six cylinders of an internal combustion engine. With foot and hand, I put the revolving crank shaft in touch with the rear wheels and proceed to pilot the whole mechanism to the station, passing or halting before three sets of automatic signal lights as I go. At the station, I cease operating machinery and resign myself to another man's operation of an enormous secondary mover, fed by a third rail from a hydroelectric turbine at Niagara Falls. I cannot glance out of the window without seeing a steamboat on the Hudson River, a steam shovel on the speculative real estate development, a travelling crane on a coal dock, or a file of motor cars on any street. Every so often comes the faint roar and silver glint of an airplane, winging its way above the river.

Arrived at the metropolitan terminal, I buy a pack of cigarettes by depositing a coin in a machine which hands me matches and says, 'Thank you'. I then spend ten minutes walking just three blocks. If I tried to shorten this time appreciably, I should most certainly be killed by a machine. Instead, I look down into an enormous pit where the day before yesterday, according to the best of my recollection, there stood a solid brownstone house. Now it is an inferno of swarming men, horses, trucks, pile drivers, rock drills, steam shovels, clacking pumps, and preparation for erecting a gigantic steel derrick. From across the street comes the deafening rat-tat of riveters.

I enter my office building and a machine shoots me vertically towards the roof. I step into a large room, stopping for a moment on the threshold to sort out the various mechanical noises which lend a never-ending orchestral accompaniment to all my working hours in town. The sputter of typewriters, the thud as the carriage is snapped back; the alternate rings and buzzes of the telephone switchboard; the rhythmic thump of the adding machine; the soft grind of a pencil sharpener; the remorseless clack of the addressograph and mimeograph. During the day I make and receive about twenty calls upon the telephone. I crank an adding machine from time to time. I may operate a typewriter for an hour or so. Meanwhile my eye can seldom stray long from my watch, if the day is to be got through with at all.

To go up or downtown I use one of the three horizontal levels of transportation which the city affords. As a profound melancholia always accompanies a trip on the lowest, I endeavour to use the upper two exclusively. Many of my fellow citizens do the same, particularly since a score of them were killed at Times Square the other day. Killed in the rush hour, like beef in the Chicago stockyards; except that the packers put nor more animals into a pen than can go in.

In the evening I reverse the morning process. At home, I may sit for a few moments beneath a machine which gives off ultra-violet rays, or I may dance to strains of a machine which runs a steel needle over a corrugated rubber disc, and for the governor of whose delicate mechanism we are indebted to James Watt. For days at home, direct contact is limited to running the motor car and making minor repairs upon it; answering the telephone; using, hearing, tinkering with the various household so-called labour-savers – particularly the plumbing system.

In the summer, by way of contrast, I may spend weeks in a mountain camp, where the only mechanisms are the motor car, the telephone, and a remarkably temperamental contrivance for pumping water. Year in year out I doubt if my direct contact with machines averages much over two hours a day. When I go to town, the ratio runs considerably higher; when I stay at home, an hour would certainly cover it; in the summer an hour would be too much.

As far as I am aware, no permanently, evil effects befall me by virtue of these two mechanical hours. I suffer from no prolonged monotonies, fatigues or repressions. The worst moments are dodging street traffic and hearing its roar, riding in the subway, changing tires and cleaning out the incinerator. When the telephone become unduly obstreperous, I go away and leave it. By far the most fatiguing noise in my office is the scraping of chair legs on the hard composition floor – and chairs I believe antedated Watt. All the depressions that I suffer from direct contact with machinery are certainly compensated for by the helping hand it holds out to me – a calculator for figuring percentages, an oil heater which requires no stoking, a reading lamp which does not have to be trimmed and filled, an elongated radius of travel possibilities, a car for errands, together with the genuine thrill which often comes from controlling its forty horses.

I do not feel like a slave, though of course I may be one all the same. Clocks and watches are hard masters but so they always have been; there is nothing new or ominous about their tyranny. No individual living in a social group is ever free, but I wonder if these two mechanised hours have put more shackles on me than were to be found on the average citizen of Rome two thousand years ago, or of China today – cultures innocent of engines both. As I look about the United States, the most mechanised nation under the sun, I have reason to believe – and later will bring in the statistical proof – that the number of those bound intimately to the rhythm of the machines is a small percentage of the total population, while there are probably more people with contacts remoter than mine than with closer contacts. In other words, I am more mechanised than the majority of my fellow citizens, and needless to say, far less mechanised than a minority thereof . . .

Questions

1 What was Stuart Chase's perspective of the relationship between science, and technology and progress?

2 What were the worst aspects of technological development that he outlined?

3 How has technology altered from the descriptions he gives for America in the 1920s to modern-day Britain?

4 In your view, has technology increasingly empowered us since the 1920s or has it increasingly controlled us?

5 Who do you think controls technological development – is it scientists and technologists or is it other individuals and groups?

Here are some multiple-choice questions.

1 Which of the following is the best example of technological development:

   a research into the cause of autism;

   b laboratory experimentation into the effects of the MMR vaccine;

   c the development of new drugs to combat AIDS;

   d observation and recording of experimental data?

2 Which of the following pieces of information about autism is most accurate:

   a the incidence of autism in the UK is falling;

   b autism has only arisen in the last 20 years;

   c autism could effect one child in 200 in the UK;

   d there is no evidence of a genetic cause for autism?

3 It could be claimed that science is neutral if:

   a it is based on clear moral values;

   b scientists are allowed to express their personal opinions;

   c science limits itself to descriptions of the laws of nature;

   d scientific investigation is financed by large corporations.

4 Which of the following is not a limitation on the neutrality of science?

   a Political interference with the results produced by scientists.

   b Differential funding in favour of scientists working for large companies.

c The deliberate suppression of some scientific 'findings'.

d Scientists seeking to find fundamental truths about the world we live in.

5 Cosmology is concerned with:

a improving ways of getting astronauts into space;

b the origin and development of the universe;

c the identification of technological improvements;

d the science of society.

6 The ratio of opticians to the overall population in Ghana is about:

a 1:20;

b 1:20 million;

c 1:4 million;

d 1:400 000.

7 The development of adaptive glasses involves all of the following except:

a alternative technology;

b science and technology;

c progress;

d neutral science and technology.

8 The development of alternative infant feeding treatments by large multinationals is an example of:

a neutral science;

b appropriate technology;

c neutral technology;

d inappropriate technology.

9 The concept of 'progress':

a is accepted by all groups in all societies;

b is based on scientific proof;

c is based on value judgements;

d is readily quantifiable using precise measures.

10 Which of the following is the best example of scientific progress:

a the development of the steam engine;

b the production of modern-day computers;

c the discovery of the laws of gravity;

d improvements in modern motor vehicles?

What do you think about the following issues now?

1 Is there such a thing as neutral science?

2 Can we say whether science and technology lead to progress?

3 If we can, what criteria would we use to measure progress?

4 Are people today better off than in the past as a result of scientific and technological development?

analyse
this

What do you think about the following issues now?

1 Is there such a thing as neutral science?

2 Can we say whether science and technology lead to progress?

3 If we can, what criteria would we use to measure progress?

4 Are people today better off than in the past as a result of scientific and technological development?

8

Nature and the environment

When Adlai Stevenson retired as US ambassador to the United Nations he said:

We travel together passengers on a little space ship, dependent upon its vulnerable reserves of air and soil, all committed for our safety to its security and peace; preserved from annihilation only by the care, and the work, and I will say the love we give to our fragile craft.

Questions

1 Do you think that the space ship analogy is an appropriate one?

2 Do you think that planet Earth is protected by the care, work and love of mankind?

3 What do we do to harm our planet?

4 Is the long-term future of the planet secure?

In the early 1970s an important book entitled *The Limits to Growth* generated much public concern and debate in the media. Newspaper headlines painted a stark picture: 'The end of civilization as we know it!'

The authors predicted that we were heading for a global catastrophe. The book was put together by a group of scientists and technologists who used computer modelling to show the impact of future trends. In particular they looked at factors that were causing increasing problems:

- increases in population;

- increasing use of non-renewable resources and

- increasing population.

key terms

carrying capacity

The 'carrying capacity' of a specific area is the maximum population of a given species that can be indefinitely maintained without a degradation of the resource base that might lead to a reduction of the population in the future.

earth

An important distinction is often drawn between the terms 'the Earth' and 'the world'. The Earth is a creation of the cosmos and is independent of man. In contrast, the world is a human artefact: it is a conceptual creation of human experience and information.

exponential

An increase which becomes more and more rapid.

cornucopian

A belief in an abundant supply. The idea is based on the Greek symbol of plenty, which is a goat's horn overflowing with flowers, fruit, and corn. ▶

Their model showed that these factors were increasing at an exponential rather than an arithmetic rate. In other words, instead of increasing 2, 4, 6, 8, 10 and so forth, they were actually increasing in an exponential fashion – 2, 4, 8, 16, 32, 64, 128, 256, 512 and so on – which quickly blows up into very big numbers.

The Club of Rome set out a number of models relating growth to carrying capacity (the ability of the planet to support its population).

If the carrying capacity of the earth were to grow exponentially and keep ahead of the growth of population and the growth of the economy then continuous growth would be possible.

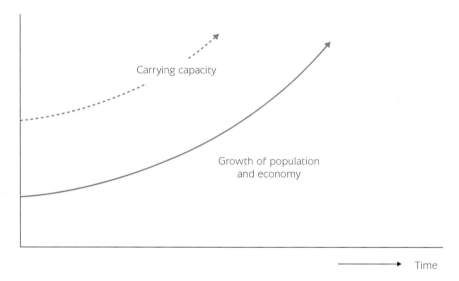

However, a more likely scenario is that responses to the environmental challenges are delayed, leading to an overshoot and to the collapse of the carrying capacity of the Earth, as illustrated below.

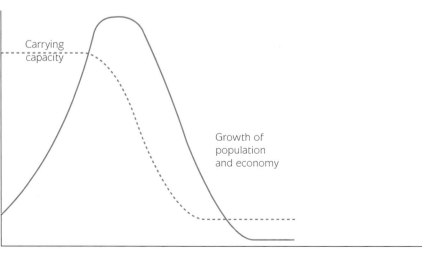

anthropocentric

Regarding humankind as the centre of existence.

species

A class of things having common characteristics.

biosphere

Regions of the earth's crust and atmosphere occupied by living organisms.

The Club of Rome therefore advocated that responses should be made to limit population and economic growth, thus enabling us to sustain life within the carrying capacity of the Earth.

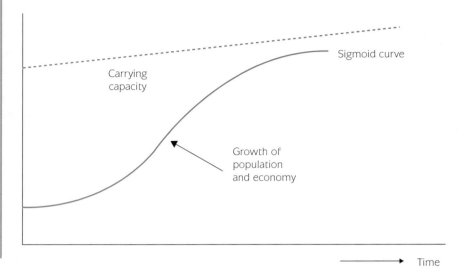

This last approach is referred to as sigmoid growth because human populations respond to exponential growth by cutting back growth into a sustainable pattern of development so that we have an S-shaped (sigmoid) growth pattern.

In the late 1990s the Club of Rome produced a follow-up book, which argued that in many ways we have already moved beyond the limits to growth, pointing to factors such as:

- rising sea levels;

- increases in temperatures on a world scale;

- increasing numbers of people living in poverty;

- the rise of international terrorism.

In the 1960s the writer Kenneth Boulding made a damning criticism of the way in which we have been living on the planet in his work *The Coming of Spaceship Earth.*

Boulding argued that we tend to live as if we are in a 'cowboy economy'. The lonesome cowboy rides across the plane, every now and then stopping to have a meal of beans. He makes a small fire, and when he has eaten he kicks over the traces of his fire, with little harm being done.

However, the problem is that we do not live in a 'cowboy economy'; rather it is more apt to think of us as space travellers, living in a 'spaceship economy'. In the spaceship there are only finite resources and we must be careful not to create too much waste and pollution because this gets in our way.

Boulding argued that we must learn to live as if we are in a finite space capsule, using resources carefully, causing as little pollution as possible and respecting the various natural systems around us.

From the 1960s people around the world have increasingly started to realize that environmental problems are a global issue rather than just a local one. In the 1960s concern about the environment became evident in a range of countries. For example:

- In Japan, a company called the Chiso Corporation allowed mercury, a by-product of its chemical processes, to seep into Minimata Bay. People began to take notice as first the fish stocks began to be depleted, and then animals such as cats that ate the fish developed convulsions and died. A number of children were born with defects. Soon a protest movement developed and the company was taken to court. Initially it denied responsibility, but gradually pressure was exerted on the company and the chairman was forced to make a humiliating public acknowledgement of responsibility and to pay compensation to the victims of the pollution.

- In America, Rachel Carson wrote her famous book *Silent Spring,* bringing to the public's attention the effects of pesticides, which were wiping out bird life and having a negative effect on the food chain. In the 1960s a group of protesters drew attention to Love Canal where new houses had been built on polluted land, leading to women miscarrying and babies being born with a number of abnormalities. Women were at the heart of the protest and eventually locked the board members of the corporation in a mobile building at Love Canal. President Kennedy praised the women's actions.

This period saw the development of Greenpeace and other environmental action groups. As groups like Greenpeace developed it was quickly realized that concern about the environment was a shared problem across the world rather than a number of local issues.

By the early 1980s representatives of various countries were coming together to discuss international environmental issues, and in 1987 the World Commission on the Environment came up with a useful definition of sustainable development, which is: 'Development which meets the needs of existing generations while at the same time furthering the interests of generations yet to come.' The notion here is that human progress can only take place when:

- we consider the needs of all of the people with whom we share the planet today;

- we consider the needs of the next generation and all succeeding generations.

In 1992 we saw the signing of the Rio Treaty on the environment, which led to the creation of Agenda 21 – an agenda of sustainable actions for nations for the twenty-first century. Agenda 21 led to the creation of many Agenda 21 local action groups, for example partnerships of schools, businesses, local government and other interested parties at a local level up and down the UK.

The Kyoto Climate Change Treaty was signed in 1997. Nations agreed to limit their production of climate-changing gases. One of the major difficulties of this treaty is that a number of countries, such as Australia and in particular the USA, have a poor record and have failed to meet the targets set.

The Rio+10 agreement was signed in Johannesburg in 2002. It sought to build on the Kyoto and Rio Treaties and is an attempt to bring all of the nations of the world together in seeking to limit environmental degradation. An important step has been the acceptance of the Rio Treaty by China and Russia, which puts pressure on the USA to comply.

■ Why care about the environment?

Most of us in the western world are well provided for so why should we care if human activities are damaging the environment? By wanting to enjoy the material benefits of a consumer society we are conceding that environmental problems are an acceptable consequence of economic progress. Of course there will be shortages of raw materials from time to time and pollution is worrying, but the ingenuity of scientists and technologists will see us through the difficult times. Food shortages can be solved easily by producing high-yielding genetically engineered crops, and should raw materials become scarce we can always mine the ocean floor or even the moon.

This cornucopian vision of an endless harvest supplied free from nature is widely believed, although we are now beginning to view our planet in a different light. As the burning of fossil fuels disturbs the earth's climate and as growing markets deplete the global stock of fish, can we really believe that there are no ecological limits? That there are limits to economic growth is now well documented and even economists are beginning to think environmentally.

However, despite the arrival of 'environmental economics', there is still too little attention given to the obvious – that economic and social development is dependent on conserving the natural world. In this regard, Kenneth Boulding was the first economist to break ranks with his profession. At the beginning of his book, *The Growth Illusion,* Douthwaite quotes Boulding as saying: 'Anyone who believes that economic growth can go on forever in a finite world is either a madman or an economist.'

So what should we do? Instead of simply not caring about the environment we should respond on the basis of enlightened self-interest. Whilst still believing that the resources of the natural world are at our disposal, we could ensure their present and future by learning to use them wisely – what economists now refer to as 'the sustainable use of resources'. This anthropocentric vision of a sustainable future is still flawed, however, because it excludes any moral consideration for the wellbeing of the natural world. Should we not be showing a deeper level of caring, one that regards the natural world as valuable in its own right, that appreciates that it deserves to be valued because it forms part of this unique interconnected web of life on our planet? It is this valuing of the Earth's natural heritage that provides many people with an environmental ethic founded on a compassionate regard for nature – one that not only responds to the effects produced by human use of material nature but also considers the values attached to nature. This means recognizing the motives behind the actions we take, which in turn affects the way we interact with our surroundings.

Does this ethic go far enough? Is there still a deeper level of caring – one that encourages people to experience the natural world rather than simply conceding value to it? This level of caring goes beyond the establishment of a moral code concerning the natural world and focuses on people's inner development and identification with various spiritual and cultural traditions. Some people believe this is, ultimately, the only way we can ensure the continued survival of life on Earth.

Human beings cannot help but use natural resources and thereby change nature. We would die if we did not do this. Nature is changed not just by human intervention in nature but also by changes by factors such as earthquakes – factors that are intrinsic to nature. However, some people are uneasy with this distinction. They argue that, because humans are a part of nature, any changes, good or bad, brought about by human activities are also intrinsic to nature. This view may lead them to condone human abuse of nature as 'only natural'. The problem with this argument is that it conveniently dodges responsibility for pressing environmental concerns that can no longer be ignored. What is at stake is the future wellbeing of life on Earth.

Fortunately, changes intrinsic to nature are no longer as dramatic as they were in the distant past. Yet earthquakes, volcanic eruptions, tornadoes, meteorites, floods and landslides show that nature is able to unleash violent forces beyond human control. Some natural changes, such as the gradual erosion of rocks wrought by wind, water and glacier action effect change over geological time and are barely discernible in a lifetime's gaze. The practised eye is more likely to note changes occurring over months and years. These include the advance and retreat of glaciers, the tidal rise and fall along our coasts and estuaries, the watery paths cut by meandering rivers, the invasion of fertile land by deserts, and the seasonal fluctuations in temperature, rainfall and the like. Some of these intrinsic changes are interconnected as when smoke from forest fires and ash from volcanoes block the sun and influence local or global weather patterns and change patterns of living.

The astonishing rise in the human population during the last 30 years undoubtedly contributes much to environmental destruction. It has all but doubled from a figure of 3.7 billion in 1970 to 6 billion in 2000 and the trend is predicted to continue before settling down to about 15 billion in the mid twenty-first century.

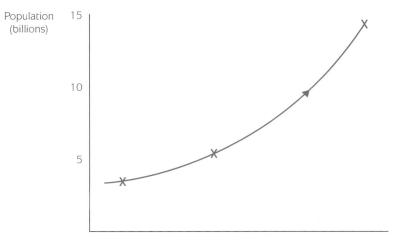

Increase in world population

This dramatic rise in population has prompted serious concerns about human impact on the Earth's life-support systems as more and more of the Earth's resources are used up and not replaced. The first person to draw popular attention to human impact on nature was Rachel Carson whose celebrated book, *Silent Spring,* documented the catastrophic decline of songbird species following increased use of pesticides. Carson's early warnings of a gathering ecological crisis brought about an examination of the long-term environmental impacts of western society's way of life, which ultimately led to a ban on the use of the pesticide DDT.

As human activities intervene more and more in nature, we have become increasingly aware that as a species we are able to set in motion changes that can cause far-reaching unwanted effects on the Earth's life-support systems. For example, it is now known that non-toxic fluorocarbon propellant in aerosol sprays destroys ozone in the Earth's upper atmosphere, a gas essential for shielding the surface of the Earth from damaging ultraviolet solar radiation. Likewise we know that overgrazing in savannah lands and the steppes removes the plants that protect the soil from the action of wind allowing desert conditions to spread as the soil is eroded and the carpet of vegetation is destroyed. The one environmental issue that has caught the public's imagination in a big way is the global effect of deforestation, particularly in the tropical rain forests. Deforestation not only removes species of animals and plants from the Earth for ever – it also reduces the transpiration of water vapour and causes far-reaching climate changes. Furthermore, each of us is responsible for global warming through the burning of fossil fuels that release carbon dioxide into the atmosphere. By increasing the absorption of thermal energy that would otherwise be radiated into outer space, carbon dioxide acts as a thermal 'blanket' trapping heat, which leads to melting ice caps, a subsequent rise in sea level and climate changes.

The effects on natural processes of some human-induced changes are not very well understood because genetic and other effects cannot be known in the short term. In Japan, environmentalists are trying to stop people from eating whale and dolphin meat by pointing out that it contains pollutants such as mercury that can kill. Once it was thought that toxic chemicals could be dumped and somehow they would go away, but the reality is that they are carried off to destinations that we would never have suspected, such as the bodies of whales and dolphins. The invisible undermining of our future by synthetic chemicals is disrupting the reproductive, immune and behaviour systems of wildlife and human beings worldwide. Variously called gender benders, xenoestrogens, copycat hormones and oestrogenic compounds, this new class of chemicals appear to be linked to defective sexual organs, behavioural abnormalities and impaired fertility in animals. Is this why male human sperm counts have dropped by as much as 50 per cent or why are women suffering from a dramatic rise in hormone-related cancers?

Humans are directly responsible for decreasing biodiversity (biological diversity). This concept has been propelled into the public consciousness by its association with a growing sense of loss; loss of familiar species such as songbirds; loss of remote species barely discovered and then exterminated; loss of cherished landscapes and habitat. Biodiversity is the total variety of life on Earth and it comprises all the species of plants and animals in the world, including their genes, the ecosystems in which they live, and the services they provide to keep the planet healthy.

Lions and tigers are examples of distinct species of animals because in the wild they do not interbreed – but they can! In captivity, when encouraged to interbreed, they produce offspring. These are called 'tiglons' when the father is a tiger, and 'ligers' when the father is a lion. So why didn't these two big cats hybridize in nature in historical times when their ranges overlapped across a large part of the Middle East and India? Well, they liked different habitats, and lions are social cats whereas tigers are solitary beasts. This discouraged the two species from meeting up and bonding long enough to produce offspring. So lions and tigers are distinct species because natural conditions prevented them from interbreeding.

'Ligers' and 'Tiglons' have been interbred in captivity

'Ecosystem' is a more complex concept than 'species' in the biological hierarchy. An ecosystem consists of a community of species and their environments functioning as a self-sustaining ecological unit in nature – or at least that is what passes as a dictionary definition of an ecosystem. Although we can describe ecosystems using the language of science, complex ecosystems such as rainforests and coral reefs have established their 'self-sustaining' dynamics independent of human influence over geological timescales that is so astonishing. It is the fact that they exist at all, a treasury of life in an all but lifeless universe. Ecosystems are more than a 'community of species' and we have yet to begin to understand their importance to life on Earth and especially to our material and spiritual wellbeing.

Wilson, in his book *Diversity of Life*, highlights some of the growing list of ecosystems comprising masses of species which are threatened, either directly by human activities such as the logging of tropical forests, or indirectly by the pollution and predation of areas such as coral reefs. Surely we need to defend them all, not just because at one level of caring we may value their 'right' to exist but because they may be useful? For example, suppose, in electing to preserve, say, five things that we wanted from nature, it turned out that the 5000 things we did not want were absolutely critical to the sustainable yield of the five? Charismatic though larger species such as lions and tigers are, these depend on, and are 'umbrellas' for, the life around them. It is the interdependency of life within an ecosystem that marks it out as such, and conservationists now focus on the preservation of entire habitats, not just the star species that reach the picture books. Ecosystems are under threat everywhere because we fail to recognize these interdependencies.

Leakey and Lewin have claimed that western civilization, with its high-tech lifestyles, has come to ignore the essential connection between the human psyche and the non-human world of nature, while emphasizing the promise of other worlds. They argue that the bond that exists between humans and nature is the result of millennia of evolution:

And it is this intimacy that enables us to place value on biodiversity of which we are a part today, separate them from the direct economic benefits of food, materials and medicines, and separate from the ecosystem services upon which our physical survival depends. The value of the species around us now reaches to the human spirit – not an easy thing to do in the context of science, but valid nonetheless. We may value biodiversity because it nurtures the human psyche, the human spirit, the human soul.

When they realize the complexity of environmental problems, people often experience acute feelings of helplessness and fear that it is already too late to 'stop the rot'. They know that human activity is rapidly unravelling ecosystems and destabilizing the natural environment with consequences that cannot be good. They know that the solution is to act far more prudently and to conserve that which through carelessness is being destroyed. Why do people find it so difficult collectively to do merely what is so obvious? Two-and-a-half thousand years ago Euripides wrote: 'We know the good, we apprehend it clearly. But we can't bring it to achievement.'

We know what is wrong with our behaviour yet as a species we seem incapable of doing anything about it. Caring about the environment is not an optional matter. It should be the primary concern of all humanity and we ignore the danger signs at our peril. Together with all the other wishes being expressed for the new century that is unfolding let us hope that caring for the environment will take on the importance that it really deserves.

■ Gaia

In 1979 the British scientist, J.E. Lovelock, produced his book *Gaia: A New Look at Life on Earth,* which developed the proposition 'that the biosphere is a self-regulating entity with the capacity to keep our planet healthy by controlling the chemical and physical environment.' Gaia, the Greek goddess of the Earth, was chosen as a convenient shorthand symbol for this idea.

If we accept this concept then our planet has an existence that is over and above the existence of man and suggests that the planet will come to survive long after we are gone. The challenge for man is not to tamper with natural forces to such an extent that we make the planet uninhabitable for ourselves. We are rapidly pushing in that direction.

■ Ecocentric and technocentric views

There are many views about the relationship we should have with the planet. Two contrasting views are:

● *technocentric;* and

● *ecocentric.*

Technocentrics are optimistic about the future of the planet because they believe that technology will provide the solutions to the problems man creates. For example, contraception and other forms of family planning provide the answer to the population explosion, and new inventions such as catalytic converters in motor vehicles enable us to use energy in a more environmentally friendly way. The technocentric believes that mankind has the intelligence to sort out problems and is particularly ingenious when the going gets tough.

In contrast, an ecocentric believes in preserving ecological systems and that we should not tamper with nature. We associate this view with 'deep ecology', the view that nature is sacred and that we should not play around with it.

You can see that people fit somewhere along a continuum between deep ecology and optimistic technocentrism. For example, supporters of Greenpeace are at the end of the ecocentric end of the continuum. People like the American President, George W. Bush, who is nicknamed 'the toxic Texan' because of his disregard for the environmental impact of such activities as opening new oilfields in Alaska, are at the technocentric end of the spectrum.

Ecocentrics argue that it is foolish to press ahead and to assume that we will come up with technological solutions to the Earth's problems because by then it will be too late.

Many people argue that we should take an anticipatory approach – think about problems before they arrive and take appropriate corrective steps. Others tend to have more of a reactive view – they are in favour of taking action when real problems occur. Where do you stand?

Questions

1 Do you think that attitudes in British society are more representative of a 'cowboy' or 'spaceship' economy?

2 Should environmental concern be primarily driven at local or at a global level?

3 Is there any hope for inter-governmental action on the environment if the world's biggest polluter, the USA, does not sign up?

4 What do you consider to be a moral view of the wellbeing of the natural world?

5 How can we develop a moral code towards the natural world?

6 In your view are 'ecosystems' more than just collections of species?

7 What is your view of Gaia?

8 Are you more technocentric or ecocentric?

Here are some multiple-choice questions.

1 Population exceeds carrying capacity when:

a a country experiences a fall in population;

b the carrying capacity of a country is rising at a faster rate than population;

c an area can carry its population into the foreseeable future;

d degradation of the resource base is resulting from population changes.

2 The book *The Limits to Growth* suggested that:

a world population is increasing in a sustainable way;

b technocentric solutions are superior to ecocentric ones;

c exponential growth of a number of factors poses a threat to survival;

d growth is being held back by not enough industrial expansion.

3 A feature of a spaceship economy is:

a unlimited availability of natural resources;

b the ability of the spaceship to cope with all forms of pollution;

c a finite quantity of scarce resources;

d astronauts who know where they are going.

4 Rachel Carson's *Silent Spring* was particularly worried about the depletion of:

a tigers;

b lions;

c fish stocks;

d bird life.

5 Agenda 21 was established by:

a the World Commission on the Environment;

b the Rio Treaty;

c the Kyoto Climate Convention;

d the Johannesburg Treaty.

6 The world's population:

a is currently about 15 billion;

b has stopped increasing;

c is due to stabilize in the middle of this century;

d is mainly concentrated in Europe and the Americas.

7 The Gaia proposition is that:

a the Earth is heading for self destruction;

b the biosphere is a self-regulating entity;

c the future of the planet is dominated by man;

d the planet was created for man.

8 George W. Bush is a good example of:

a a deep ecologist;

b Gaia;

c a technocentrist;

d a megalomaniac.

9 Ecocentrism is associated with:

a weak sustainability;

b technocentrism;

c a reactive approach to the environment;

d strong sustainability.

10 A sustainable future is most likely to be secured by:

a population increasing faster than carrying capacity;

b increases in the use of toxic chemicals;

c an anticipatory approach to environmental issues;

d the decline in biodiversity.

key terms

dredged spoil

Material dredged out of rivers and the sea edge.

inert

Without active chemical or other properties.

landfill

An area filled by the process of using waste to landscape or reclaim areas of ground.

recycling

Converting waste to reusable material.

conservation

Preservation of the natural environment.

■ The problem of waste in modern society

Waste is any substance that is no longer required. With growing numbers of people, and growing prosperity, more and more waste is being created. Waste is usually defined by the place where it is produced:

● at home – household waste;

● in factories and industry – industrial waste;

● in hospitals and clinics – clinical waste;

● on farms – agricultural waste.

It is also sometimes defined by the form it takes (liquid or solid) and sometimes by its properties (hazardous or inert). Some waste is defined by how it is dealt with, for example:

● recyclable waste;

● green waste (for composting);

● combustible waste (for burning).

It is a well-known law of physics that matter cannot be created or destroyed. We can change its physical form (solid, liquid or gas) or chemical form, but we cannot make it disappear. If you throw something away it does not disappear. It may be burned, but it is still there as gases, ash and heat. It may be buried (landfilled) so that bacteria decompose it, but that still leaves the rotted materials and produces gases. It may stay where it is, but it will not disappear.

Government statistics show that in 2000 about 420 million tonnes of waste were produced in the UK, arising in the following ways.

Type of waste	Million tonnes
Agricultural waste	80
Mining and quarry waste	74
Construction and demolition waste	70
Industrial waste	69
Dredged spoil	51
Sewage sludge	35
Household waste	26
Commercial waste	15

Source: HMSO Digest of Environmental Statistics, 2000.

© Crown copyright

Agricultural waste is made up of all of the parts of crops that are not used in food processing – for example the stalks and husks of wheat, the non-root part of sugar beet and so forth.

Animal farming also creates waste, and here the waste can be used as an organic fertilizer on the soil. Practices such as farmers burning the corn stubble in their fields have been banned because this adds to atmospheric pollution.

Mining and quarrying produce huge piles of unwanted materials, for example in the form of unsightly coal stacks. Today this is less of a problem because coal mining has gone into decline and many of the former pit heaps have been planted with trees and grass to hide them.

Industrial waste appears in a number of forms including solids and liquids requiring different types of processing. There are clear rules and guidelines about how this can be disposed of – for example what materials are allowed to go into particular types of drains.

The environment protection and the pollution prevention and control regulations have placed legal obligations on businesses and the processes that they carry out. For example, all companies involved in wood treatment need to have a permit that sets out strict controls on the releases from these processes and lays down conditions for monitoring and record keeping. There are also strict controls on waste under a 'duty of care' for businesses. All industrial wastes must be identified, and documented and only transported by carriers that are authorised to do so. There are additional regulations for special wastes such as toxic materials. In addition the Water Resources Act 1991 protects 'controlled waters', which include rivers, lakes, coastal seas and groundwater. It is an offence for businesses to discharge wastes into these controlled waters without consent (which sets out the types, limits and outlets into which waste can be discharged). There are also controls on what can be put down the sink and into drains. Businesses that fail to comply are faced with heavy fines and, in the worst cases, prison sentences. Firms can also be prosecuted for failing to minimize the material that they use in packaging for their products.

Sewage sludge consists of people's bodily waste as well as some industrial waste that is allowed to go into drains. Today only treated sewage is allowed to go into rivers and into the sea. The Environment Agency is responsible for monitoring this to check that water quality is maintained.

Hazardous waste is controlled by the Environment Protection Act 1997. Wastes that are a danger to health are termed 'special wastes' and they must be treated in a carefully set out way.

Municipal solid waste is waste that is collected from street cleaning, or taken in dustbin sacks from people's houses, and which is deposited by people at the local tip.

You are all familiar with household waste, consisting of old newspapers and magazines, food packets, left-over food, bottles and so forth.

The breakdown of a typical household's weekly waste is shown in the table below.

Type of waste	%	
Newspapers, magazines, etc.	18	
Paper and board	5	
Plastic bottles and pots	4	
Plastic wrappings	2	
Plastic non-packaging	5	
Textiles	3	
Glass bottles and jars	6	
Ferrous metal food and drink cans	3	
Non-ferrous cans, containers and closures	1	
Other metal	1	
Kitchen and garden waste	44	(however, this is highly seasonal)
Other (shoes, stones, plant pots, dust)	8	

■ Ways of treating waste

In this country much municipal and industrial waste is buried in holes in the ground through the process of landfilling. Before this happens the waste is typically treated to reduce its volume. This is mainly done by:

● compacting the waste – using compacting machinery like you see on the back of a dustbin lorry;

● taking out some of the materials – glass, paper and so forth – for recycling;

● composting;

● incineration (burning).

In this country we depend very much on landfill, but new European Union regulations are going to require large amounts of municipal biodegradable waste to be diverted from landfill by 2016. The figure shows how municipal solid waste was treated and disposed of in the UK in 2000.

At present the national recycling target is 25 per cent, but you can see that we are well short of that figure. There are all sorts of recycling schemes for:

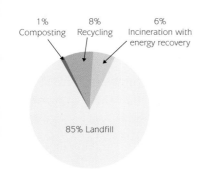

1% Composting   8% Recycling   6% Incineration with energy recovery

85% Landfill

The 'treatment' of municipal waste

141

- paper;
- glass;
- old clothes;
- toys;
- CDs and tapes.

Composting of kitchen and garden wastes involves turning them into compost or soil conditioner, either in your own back garden or at a central point.

Because incinerators produce electricity, steam or hot water, they are usually called energy-from-waste (EFW) plants. Burning waste in this way can help to generate substantial amounts of electricity.

Incineration turns the waste into carbon dioxide, water vapour and small amounts of other gases, leaving an ash residue which is landfilled. Some of the gases can be harmful and are not allowed to escape into the atmosphere.

Landfill sites are often disused pits or worked-out quarries where minerals such as sand, gravel, clay or chalk have been excavated. Filling these pits with waste enables the land to be restored over time.

In 1996 the government introduced the landfill tax, which is a tax on business based on the amount of waste created. It is designed to encourage business to develop new ways of recycling waste rather than sending it for landfill. The government has also thought about ways of encouraging householders to produce less waste. At one time it was considering a tax on the number of bin bags created per household, but it has decided this would be too expensive to administer.

Questions

1 Disposed of needles and syringes are an example of:

a agricultural waste;

b domestic waste;

c clinical waste;

d household waste.

2 Toxic substances would be an example of:

a inert waste;

b hazardous waste;

c green waste;

d combustible waste.

3 Cans, bottles and newspapers are examples of:

a organic waste;

b recyclable waste;

c green waste;

d liquid waste.

4 Roughly what percentage of UK waste is in the form of agricultural waste:

a 20 per cent;

b 30 per cent;

c 40 per cent;

d 50 per cent?

5 Bodily waste is typically disposed of as:

a household waste;

b dredged spoil;

c demolition waste;

d sewage sludge.

6 Which of the following is true?

a Special wastes can be disposed of in ordinary drains.

b Animal waste cannot be recycled for productive use.

c Firms can be prosecuted for using too much packaging.

d Household waste creates the greatest amount of waste in the UK.

7 The body responsible for checking on water quality in this country is:

a the Environment Agency;

b municipal authorities;

c the Pollution Prevention Agency;

d the Water Resources Agency.

8 Which of the following accounts for the greatest proportion of household waste:

a plastic bottles and pots;

b glass bottles and jars;

c paper and board;

d textiles?

9 Which of the following is not an example of municipal solid waste:

a materials collected from street cleaning;

b dustbin sacks collected from houses;

c chemical containers collected from firms;

d junk deposited at the local tip by householders?

10 Which of the following types of waste is most likely to vary in quantity during the year:

a plastic bottles;

b ferrous metal food and drink cans;

c textiles;

d kitchen and garden waste?

11 Which of the following is the most commonly used type of treating and disposing of waste in this country:

a recycling;

b landfill;

c composting;

d incineration?

12 An energy-from-waste plant is primarily responsible for:

a compacting waste materials;

b producing electricity, steam or hot water;

c landfill operations;

d composting of garden wastes.

■ The problem of pollution in modern society

A pollutant is any substance introduced into the environment that adversely affects the usefulness of a resource. Some of the most dramatic effects of pollution have been experienced in the USA, for example:

● when the Cuyahoga River in Ohio became so polluted that it twice caught on fire from oil floating on its surface;

● New York City was blanketed by heavy smog in the 1960s.

Nearer to home we have been aware of environmental pollution, for example when the *Torrey Canyon* oil tanker broke open to pour millions of gallons of oil onto our beaches during the late 1960s. Everyday examples of pollution include:

- air pollution from cars and industrial plant, leading to asthma and other respiratory problems;

- killing of fish and birds by toxic chemical discharges, including organic fertilizer, into water;

- household refuse being dumped or burned to form dangerous particles in the air.

Compared with 25 years ago, air quality in this country is much improved although pollution is sometimes still obvious – traffic fumes in cities like London and ozone levels that irritate the eyes and lungs. Water pollution has also notably improved, but just because a river or inland waterway does not smell, or because there are no visible signs of pollution, this does not mean that there are not life-threatening chemicals in the water.

Man's pollution involves putting synthetic (artificial) chemicals into water and airflows to combine with those that are already there naturally. Anthropogenic chemicals may result in all sorts of negative effects such as reducing bird reproduction or causing tumours in fish. The problem is that whereas humans and animals are readily able to break down natural chemicals, they are far less efficient at breaking down artificial polychlorinated chemicals such as the pesticide dichlorodiphenyl-trichloroethane (DDT). In Europe and America these chemicals have been banned.

Types of chemicals and pollutants

There are two major types of chemicals – organic and inorganic (mineral) chemicals. A third, less common, category is organometallic chemicals.

Organic chemicals

A common use of the term organic is to say that it is natural – for example, organic farming. However, we use the term 'organic' in a more technical way to refer to the fact that a chemical contains one carbon atom and usually more. One family of organic chemicals – the hydrocarbons – contain only the elements carbon and hyrdrogen.

Organic chemicals are synthesized in nature by micro-organisms, plants and animals. Examples of organic chemicals are:

- sucrose – common table sugar, which is derived from sugar cane or from sugar beet;

- acetic acid – the chemical that gives vinegar its bite.

key terms

ppm

Parts per million.

ppb

Parts per billion (one thousand times smaller than ppm).

ppt

Parts per trillion (one million times smaller than ppm).

ppq

Parts per quadrillion (one billion times smaller than ppm).

respiratory problems

Difficulties with breathing/lung problems.

synthesized

Built into a whole by combining the various elements.

toxin

This is a substance that can cause adverse effects in a plant, animal, or human and is produced by living organisms, micro-organisms, plants, insects, spiders or snakes. ▶

> ▶ **hazardous**
>
> A hazardous substance may be toxic, corrosive, reactive, flammable, radioactive or infectious, or a combination of these.
>
> **xenobiotic chemicals**
>
> Foreign chemicals that do not occur naturally in the body.

Many organic chemicals contain a large part that is natural. Chemists then work with the raw product to turn it into something that has more useful applications – for example, turning hydrocarbons into aircraft and motor vehicle fuel.

Inorganic chemicals

These typically do not contain carbon. Examples are:

- sodium hydroxide – caustic soda;
- sodium chloride – table salt;
- chlorine-containing chemicals – found in household bleaches.

Some inorganic chemicals, including many of the metals in our diet, provide us with essential nutrients, which are required for the smooth production of proteins and other biochemicals in the body.

Organometallic chemicals

These contain both an organic and an inorganic component – for example, methylmercury, which is a common water pollutant. The methyl is organic and the mercury is inorganic. Many of these chemicals are produced naturally in plants and animals, for example the blood protein haemoglobin.

Types of pollution

The following table sets out the main categories of pollution.

Category and examples	Organic or inorganic?
Organic pollutants: PCBs – polychlorinated biphenyls. These are chlorinated chemicals. Oil is another example of an organic pollutant – which becomes harmful in the form of oil spills.	
Inorganic pollutants: A common pollutant is the synthetic plant nutrients found in fertilisers. Nitrate is a good example and it is immediately harmful to human health. The nitrogen and sulphur acids found in acid rain are also inorganic pollutants. Salt can also be harmful when too much appears in water. Metals are another form of dangerous pollutant, e.g. arsenic which appears naturally can run into water supplies.	Salt and nitrate are inorganic. Metals may exist as organometallic pollutants.

Acid pollutants:	Sulphuric, nitric and hyrdrochloric acids are inorganic.
Sulphuric acid and nitric acid are the most common, being found in acid rain. Acids often run off from mining sites into water supplies.	
Physical pollutants:	Soil and garbage are a mixture of organic and inorganic components.
Any solid material found where it is not wanted. Household waste or litter on city streets is an obvious example.	
Radiological pollutants:	Radium and radon are inorganic.
Radioactive chemicals found naturally in rocks, water and the soil. For example radon and radium appear naturally in rocks and water in Cornwall.	
Biological pollutants or pathogens:	Living organisms are largely organic but do contain inorganic components.
Pathogenic micro-organisms are a serious concern – infectious bacteria, viruses and protozoa. Micro-organisms are found naturally in soiled water, air and food, and in our bodies. However, when they appear in sewage or animal waste or rotting food they can cause problems.	

The effects of pollution

The effects of pollution can be illustrated by looking at the effect of toxins on the body's organs.

- *Skin.* Corrosive acids can harm the skin. Irritant chemicals may cause reddening, swelling or itching. Detergents contain toxins that irritate the skin and many people have to wear gloves for washing up and cleaning. The metal nickel can also act as an irritant to many people when worn as jewellery. Some people develop allergies which grow in severity with increased exposure to given toxins.

- *Lungs.* Some chemicals have a local effect on the lungs including the reactive gases ozone, ammonia and chlorine, which can all harm the lungs. Silica, asbestos, coal, cotton dust and talcum powder can all be harmful to the lungs.

- *Liver.* The liver is responsible for the detoxification of xenobiotic chemicals. It is the first organ in the body to receive material from the intestine, so it receives it in a more toxic form than other organs. If the liver is exposed to higher levels of a toxin than it can detoxify, it can be damaged. Examples of chemicals that can damage the liver are carbon tetrachloride and chloroform. An excess of ethyl alcohol can cause cirrhosis of the liver.

● *Kidneys.* The kidneys also detoxify chemicals, although their major function is to filter the blood to eliminate waste products into urine while retaining water and nutrients. Mercury, cadmium and lead are all harmful to the kidneys.

● *Central nervous system.* The brain requires high levels of oxygen to function normally. Any substance that reduces oxygen is toxic to the brain. Examples include carbon monoxide and some pesticides.

● *Reproductive system.* Teratogens are chemicals that can kill the embryo or foetus or cause other damaging changes that result in mental retardation, deformed organs or other birth defects. The embryo (the foetus during the stage from about the second to the eighth week of pregnancy) is especially sensitive to teratogens. The nutrient vitamin A is a teratogen and must not be taken in excess. Pregnant women are advised to avoid exposure to alcohol, tobacco and almost all drugs because of their teratogen components.

● *Immune system.* The immune system, made up of cells, tissues and organs, seeks to get rid of foreign bodies including micro-organisms and cancer cells.

Questions

1 Which of the following is banned in the USA and Europe:

a aspirin;

b hydrocarbons;

c dichlorodiphenyltrichloroethane;

d sucrose?

2 Common table sugar is an example of:

a an inorganic chemical;

b an acid;

c an organic chemical;

d an organometallic chemical?

3 An organic chemical typically contains:

a non-natural elements;

b one or more carbon atoms;

c no carbon;

d inert material.

4 Which of the following is a hyrdrocarbon:

a salt;

b nitrates;

c oil;

d metals?

5 Household bleaches contain a high concentration of:

a chlorine;

b methylmercury;

c salt;

d radon?

6 Which of the following is a dangerous inorganic metal-based substance:

a water;

b arsenic;

c carbon;

d chlorine?

7 Which of the following is a natural based radioactive chemical found in rocks and water:

a radar;

b radox;

c radon;

d rodeo?

8 Carbon monoxide poisoning is likely to lead to all of the following except:

a a dangerous loss of oxygen to the brain;

b red blotchy patches on the skin;

c respiratory difficulties;

d increased levels of toxins in the body.

9 Which is the first organ of the body that would receive xenobiotic chemicals from the intestine:

a heart;

b lungs;

c kidneys;

d liver?

10 To reduce the risk from teratogens pregnant women should avoid excess use of all of the following during early pregnancy except:

a vitamin A;

b alcohol;

c cigarettes;

d drinking water.

11 Cirrhosis of the liver results from:

a vitamin A consumption;

b excess quantities of alcohol;

c toxic allergies;

d nickel jewellery.

12 Which of the following is least likely to be harmful to the lungs:

a smoking;

b petrol fumes;

c asbestos;

d oxygen?

Here are some more general questions for you to consider:

1 Do you think that the analogy of the Earth as a space ship is a good one?

2 Do you think that people generally treat the Earth as a space ship?

3 Do you think that the problems of waste and pollution are likely to increase?

4 Are you in favour of an anticipatory or reactive approach to the environment?

9

Mathematical reasoning and its application

Mathematical reasoning is required in most, if not all, subject areas whether we are concerned with statistical surveys in the social science, mathematical calculations in physics and chemistry or geometrical surveys in astronomy.

This chapter therefore gives you a brief guide to some of the most important mathematical techniques that will help you in your examination as well as in your everyday life and work. It does not provide a comprehensive coverage of all the mathematical techniques that you will be tested on but it does give an easy-to-understand coverage of points with which students often struggle and that are of most use in applying mathematical techniques.

■ Simple functions and their graphs

A function is a variable quantity regarded in relation to another or others in terms of which it may be expressed or on which its value depends.

For example, we could show that the amount of money spent on consumer goods each week by an 'average' household is a function of how much income the people in that household earn (as well as other factors). (In this case the variable consumer spending depends on the value of household income.)

We could express this mathematically as:
$C = fY$

Where:
C is consumer spending;
Y is household income;
f expresses the functional relationship.

If for example, the relationship was found to be:
C = 2/3Y

then we would be able to calculate that a household:

- earning £300 would spend £200 on consumption: £200 = 2/3 £300;

- earning £1000 would spend £666.66 on consumption: £666.66 = 2/3 £1000;

- earning £3000 would spend £2000 on consumption: £2000 = 2/3 £3000, and so forth.

A useful way of thinking about functions is to think of them as a rule used to convert (map) 'input' values to 'output' values.

This can be explained in terms of an input-output model, in which inputs are converted to outputs by means of a process (rule). The three components are thus:

- input;

- process;

- output.

For example, if we examine the following:

$f(x) = x^2$

The rule of this function is to square *x*. Thus the input is *x*, the rule is square it, and the output is x^2.

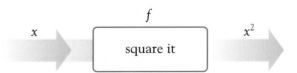

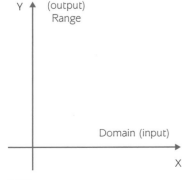

We use the term 'domain' to describe the terms that can be put into a function, and the term 'range' to describe the values that can be output from the function. Functions can thus be set out in a graphical form showing the domain as the *x* values and the range as the *y* values.

Every function *f* relates an input value *x* to an output value *f(x)*. As a result of this the function can be used to generate ordered pairs of numbers in the form:

(x,f(x))

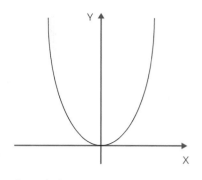

A parabola

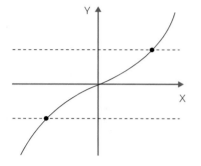

A 'one-one' function

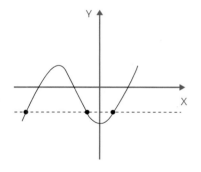

A 'many-one' function

Each ordered pair generated from the function can then be plotted against a pair of axes to produce the graph of the function. For example, the function f with output:

$$F(x) = x^2,$$

can be used to generate the collection of ordered pairs of the form:

$$(x, x^2)$$

When these are plotted they produce the graph shown on the left, which is referred to as a parabola and is obtained by plotting a number of isolated points and joining the points together by the smooth curve shown.

A one-one function, $f(x)$ is one where for every value of $f(x)$ there exists only one corresponding value of x. A many-one function $f(x)$, is a function that, for some values of $f(x)$, there exists more than one corresponding value for x.

You can quickly spot whether a function is a one-one function or a many-one function by looking at the graph and seeing if, when you draw a horizontal line, it cuts the graph just once or more than once.

An inverse function $f^1(x)$ is one that 'undoes' what $f(x)$ has done. The function $f(x)$ must be a one-one function to have an inverse.

Sometimes we may want to restrict the domain to a smaller collection of numbers than the total number that could be processed. This is called a restrictive domain.

■ Exponential growth and decay

Understanding the nature of exponential functions gives us an important understanding of many relationships in the real world. Many quantities grow or decay in a way that depends on their initial size – for example, when people catch colds as a result of having been exposed to a virus, and the virus finds conditions in the body that encourage very rapid growth. Viruses increase in number more rapidly as there are more of them in the bloodstream, so the number of viruses explodes, giving us cold symptoms – a sneeze, a runny nose, and so forth.

If it takes one day for the number of viruses in our body to double, then:

- after one week there will be 128;

- after two weeks 16 384;

- after three weeks 2.1 million;

- after four weeks 268 million, and so forth.

Fortunately viruses will also decay in an exponential way once the body or appropriate drugs are put to good use in attacking them.

There are all sorts of things in nature that have the power to rise exponentially – for example, the number of locusts in a swarm, or even the rise in human population (where birth control techniques are not put in practice).

Exponential numbers are thus numbers that rise to a power, for example numbers that then rise or fall in a progression that is squared, or cubed or increased or decreased by some other power.

In an exponential function the input variable is the power. For example, we can illustrate the function *f* with output:

$f(x) = 2^x$

x	−3	−2	−1	0	1	2	3
f(x)	$2^{-3}=⅛$	$2^{-2}=¼$	$2^{-1}=½$	$2^0=1$	$2^1=2$	$2^2=4$	$2^3=8$

Plotting these points onto a graph with a smooth curve gives the following:

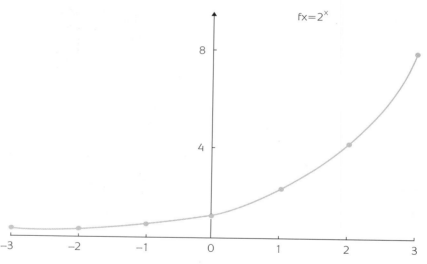

Exponential change

Nowhere is the output zero or negative. The curve crosses the vertical axis at f (0) = 1, and as x increases the exponential curve also increases without bound. You can imagine that if we continued it a little bit further it would rapidly start hitting some very big numbers – which is why we have only plotted a few points onto our page.

■ Pythagoras' theorem and trigonometry

Geometry is the branch of mathematics concerned with the properties and relations of points, lines, surfaces and solids. As such it is very useful in surveying, and also in astronomy for working out the position, movement and relationship of stars and other objects that may be billions of miles away from our planet. Trigonometry is a key part of geometry as illustrated by Pythagoras' theorem.

This theorem is usually associated with the Greeks of around 550 BC. However, recent research tends to indicate that knowledge of this theorem has been around for much longer and was known widely in both Europe and China from about 1000 BC.

Pythagoras' theorem is simply that, in a right-angle triangle, the square of the hypotenuse equals the sum of the squares of the other two sides.

The hypotenuse is the side opposite the right angle. We can illustrate this by showing that a square under the hypotenuse is equal to squares drawn off the other two sides summed together.

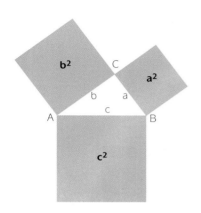

Phythagoras' theorem

From the illustration you can see that:

$$c^2 + 2ab = (a + b)^2$$

Subtracting $2ab$ from both sides, we get $c^2 = a^2 + b^2$. It is believed that Egyptian surveyors made right angles by forming a 3:4:5 triangle from a rope with 13 knots, because:

$$5^2 = 4^2 + 3^2$$

Trigonometry is that part of geometry that is concerned with similar triangles. For example, suppose that we have a wall that needs to be supported by a triangular wooden prop. We know that the wood available for the vertical prop is 4 m long and we have a piece that is 3 m long for the horizontal prop. We need to work out how long the prop needs to be for the hypotenuse side of the triangle. In order to do this we can draw a scaled-down drawing on a piece of paper drawing a triangle that is similar to the one that is required. On our paper we can use centimetres rather than metres. By doing this we can see (in our similar triangle) that the piece that is missing is 5 cm long – we need a piece of wood 5 m long. If we know the ratios of the sides of our little triangle, 5:4:3, we can predict that our similar big triangle will have the same ratios. These ratios are called the trigonometric ratios and are defined using the right-angled triangle.

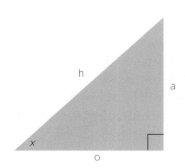

Right-angled triangle

The right-angled triangle shown on the left helps us to illustrate the three trigonometric ratios.

It possesses a right angle and an angle x. The side *opposite* to x is labelled o, the side *adjacent* to x is labelled a and the *hypotenuse* is labelled h. We can then define the three trigonometric ratios.

- Sine – the sine of the angle x is defined as the ratio o/h:

  i.e. $\sin(x) = \dfrac{o}{h}$

- Cosine – the cosine of the angle x is defined as the ratio a/h:

  i.e. $\cos(x) = \dfrac{a}{h}$

- Tangent – the tangent of the angle x is defined as the ratio of the sine and the cosine:

  i.e. $\tan(x) = \dfrac{\sin(x)}{\cos(x)}$

  $\qquad\quad = \dfrac{o}{a}$

■ Statistical measures and probability

Averages

We use the term average in our everyday conversations – for example, 'the average male thinks about sex once every five seconds'. This does not mean that every male thinks about sex as frequently – some may think about it every 20 seconds, while others think about it every second. However, we realized that five seconds is a good indicator of the time frequency for men to think about sex.

However, when we use the term average in mathematics we may be using it in one of three different ways. These three approaches to averaging are:

- the mean;
- the median; and
- the mode.

The mean

The mean is the most commonly used mathematical measure of average – and is what is generally referred to when people talk about averages. It is calculated by totalling all the values in a dataset; this total is then divided by the number of values that make up the dataset. For example, if we wanted to find out the mean amount earned by five students from part-time work in 2002, each week, we could start out by setting out a table like the one shown below:

Weekly earnings of five students in 2002:

Chris	£100
Tony	£100
Pritesh	£80
Minesh	£60
Sam	£60
Total	£400

In order to find the mean weekly wage, the total amount £400 is divided by the number of students (five) which equals £80. The mean is thus equal to the sum of the individual values in the dataset, divided by the number of values in the dataset.

The mean is a good measure of the average when a dataset contains values that are relatively evenly spread with no exceptionally high or low values – this was the case with the five students listed above.

If there are a small number of extreme numbers in a dataset then it may not be sensible to use the mean because the extreme numbers have a distorting effect. For example this might be the case if one student earned £500, or another received nothing.

The median

The median refers to the middle value in a dataset, when the values arranged in order of magnitude from smallest to largest or vice-versa. Where there are odd numbers of values in the dataset the middle value is straightforward to find. When there are equal number of values, the midpoint between the two central values is the median. For example if the weekly earnings of seven students were:

£100 £100 £90 (£80) £70 £60 £60

The median in the above is £80 – the fourth value from the start and the fourth value from the end. However, if there were eight students in the sample, then

£100 £100 £90 £80 – £70 £60 £60 £50

The median lies between £80 and £70, namely £75.

The median is a good measure of the average value when the data include exceptionally high or low values because these have little influence on the outcome. The median is the most suitable measure of average for data classified on an ordinal scale (set out in order). The median is also easy to calculate.

The mode

The mode is the most popular number in the dataset – the number that appears with the greatest frequency. It is representative or typical because it is the most common value. There may be more than one mode in a dataset if several values are equally common; alternatively there may be no mode.

The following dataset shows the number of goals scored by Manchester United in all competitions over a three-month period in 2002:

0 1 1 2 2 2 3 3 3 3 3 3 4 4 4 5 5

You can see in this example that three is the mode because it appears seven times.

The mode is the only measure of average that can be used with nominal data. For example, users of a school library were classified as 30 per cent science students, 10 per cent mathematics students and 50 per cent arts and literature students. In this case no mean or median can be calculated but art and literature students are the mode as this is the most common category.

The range and the inter-quartile range

In working with statistics it is often important to examine the dispersion of sets of figures – are figures clustered around the average, or are they widely dispersed?

We use the *range* to identify the difference between the highest and lowest figure. For example in a test involving 12 pupils, scores were (out of 100):

50 55 57 60 65 68 72 75 80 82 85 90

The range is therefore 40 marks: from 50 to 90.

The inter-quartile range is another important measure that is used in statistics because it indicates the extent to which the central 50 per cent of values within a dataset are dispersed.

In the same way that the median divides a dataset into two halves, it can be further divided into quarters by identifying the upper and lower quartiles. The lower quartile is found a quarter of the way along a dataset when the values have been arranged in order of magnitude; the upper quartile is found three-quarters of the way along the dataset. Therefore, the upper quartile lies half way between the median and the highest value in the dataset whilst the lower quartile lies halfway between the median and the lowest value in the dataset. The interquartile range is found by subtracting the lower quartile from the upper quartile.

For example, the exam marks for 20 students in a science test are arranged in order of magnitude:

43 48 50 50 52 53 56 58 59 60 62 65 66 68 70 71 74 76 78 80

The median lies at the mid-point between the two central values (tenth and eleventh) = half-way between 60 and 62 = 61.

The lower quartile lies at the mid-point between the fifth and sixth values, half-way between 52 and 53, or 52.5.

The upper quartile lies at the mid-point between the 15th and 16th values, half-way between 70 and 71, or 70.5.

The inter-quartile range for this dataset is therefore 52.5 to 70.5, which is 18, whereas the range is 43 to 80, or 37.

Probability

In statistical terms, probability means the relative frequency of occurrence in a long series of trials of the event of interest. For example, if a new bread roll has been extensively test-marketed across the UK, and it is found that seven out of 10 people like it, then it is likely that if an additional person is interviewed the probability of this person liking the roll will be seven out of 10 and that seven out of 10 people in the total UK population will like the new roll (provided we have done our sampling correctly).

Another way of defining probability is: 'The extent to which an event is likely to occur, measured by the ratio of the favourable cases to the whole number of cases possible.'

To find the probability of an event (where there is previous experience to draw on), you must predict the relative frequency of the event of interest. This can be done by considering all equally likely outcomes, so that the probability can be calculated by a simple ratio.

For example, in monopoly if a player has to throw a double to get out of jail, there are 36 possible outcomes:

(1,1) (1,2) (1,3) (1,4) (1,5) (1,6)
(2,1) **(2,2)** (2,3) (2,4) (2,5) (2,6)
(3,1) (3,2) **(3,3)** (3,4) (3,5) (3,6)   Of the 36 possibilities, only the 6
(4,1) (4,2) (4,3) **(4,4)** (4,5) (4,6)   shown in bold represent doubles.
(5,1) (5,2) (5,3) (5,4) **(5,5)** (5,6)
(6,1) (6,2) (6,3) (6,4) (6,5) **(6,6)**

The probability of throwing a double is thus 6/36, which works out as 1/6. In words, this ratio can be expressed as 'the number of ways an event of interest can occur/total number of equally likely outcomes'.

A lot of people want to know about probabilities, for example:

● a gambler wants to know the chances of winning a bet;

● astronomers want to calculate the chances of finding life on other planets;

● parents want to know the chance of having a boy or girl;

● investors want to know the chance of making a return on their investment.

Probability distribution

In calculating probability it is helpful to list all the possible outcomes in a given situation. The listed outcomes need to be mutually exclusive and exhaustive (including all possible outcomes of this type).

For example, in carrying out a scientific experiment the possible error outcomes can be set down as:

Errors of:

0	to less than 0.3
0.3	to less than 0.6
0.6	to less than 0.9

In this example, an error of 0.2 could only be recorded in the category 0 to less than 0.3. All recordings of less than 0.3 are recorded in the category 0 to less than 0.3.

Experimentation over time may have shown the following probabilities of different size experimental errors occurring:

Variable (X) (size of error)	Probability
0 to less than 0.3	5/10
0.3 to less than 0.6	3/10
0.6 to less than 0.9	2/10
	Total 1

By observing relative frequencies of past events we can convert this to probabilities for the future, assuming that the past is a representative guide to future probabilities.

This point can be illustrated by setting out absolute frequency distributions, relative frequency distributions and probability distributions for the numbers of customers logging on to a book-selling website during quarter-of-an-hour periods, over peak periods. In total, 100 periods (of 15 minutes) were surveyed involving peak hours. The purpose of the survey was to identify the probability of large numbers logging on to the website during peak periods in the future.

The table shows that, for example, between zero and five customers logged on to the site 10 times (absolute frequency) making up one-tenth of the observations (relative frequency), giving a probability of 0.10 of this happening in future Christmas periods:

The problem, however, in calculating probabilities for the future is that often they involve new situations. For example, although we have previous evidence about the frequency of people logging on to a website, this pattern may change in the future.

Absolute frequency distribution		Relative frequency distribution		Probability distribution	
variable	frequency	variable	relative frequency	variable	probability
0–5	10	0–5	10/100	0–5	0.10
6–10	15	6–10	15/100	6–10	0.15
11–20	15	11–20	15/100	11–20	0.15
21–30	10	21–30	10/100	21–30	0.10
31–40	20	31–40	20/100	31–40	0.20
41–50	30	41–50	30/100	41–50	0.30

The relative frequency definition of probability is that *if, in a large number of trials, n, r of these trials result in event E, the probability of event E is r/n.* Here is a useful formula for probability:

$$P\ (E) = \frac{r}{n}$$

P is the probability

E is the event

n is the number of trials

r is the result of the trials producing the event E.

Probabilities have values between 0 and 1. For example a probability of 0.5 represents the probability of a 5/10 chance of an event happening. If something is certain to happen, in other words when $r = n$, the probability will be 1 (for example the probability that Christmas will fall on 25 December).

We can convert a probability to a percentage by multiplying it by 100. So a probability of 5/10 represents 50 per cent.

■ Percentages

Percentage means parts out of 100 and is the same as a fraction with a denominator (bottom) of 100. Therefore, 10 per cent means 10 parts out of 100 and is the same as the fraction 10/100.

Calculating percentage change

Percentages are very useful to quantify change. This is because they provide a result in the form of parts per hundred, which is usually more readily understandable and comparable than when the information is presented as raw values. For example, let us examine the results of three students in a science class, who do tests twice a year. The results were as follows: (the results are out of 100)

	Autumn result	Summer result
Sunil	50	75
Jack	80	60
Sumaya	60	90

We can calculate the change in Sunil's mark between autumn and summer in the following way:

- determine the difference between the value in the autumn and the value in the summer – a change of 25;

- express the difference as a fraction of the starting value (50): 25/50;

- multiply by 100; this gives you the figure for the % change:

$$\frac{25}{50} \times \frac{100}{1} = 50\%$$

Using this method you should now be able to see that Jack's mark has changed by 25 per cent, and Sumaya's by 50 per cent.

Calculating percentage increase or reductions

In the previous example, the percentage change between two values was calculated. The reverse process is where the actual amount represented by a particular percentage is to be calculated. Typical examples of the use of percentages in this way are in shop sales, where the prices have been reduced by a certain percentage, or bank charges where interest rates are expressed as a percentage. Again, the use of the term 'percentage' expresses the amount in terms of parts per hundred. For example, a bank interest rate of 5 per cent is the same as saying the interest on each £1 invested is five parts out of 100 or 5p. A sale reduction of 10 per cent means that an item will be reduced by 10p for every £1 that it originally costs.

There are two ways of calculating the new value of the item following a percentage increase or reduction. For example you may wish to calculate the sale price of a ghetto blaster normally priced at £180 that has been reduced by 10 per cent.

The first method is to calculate the amount by which the item has been reduced:

10% of £180 = 10 ÷ 100 × £180 = £18

This amount is then subtracted from the original price:

£180 – £18 = £162

The second method is to calculate the percentage of the original price you are now paying for the item:

100% (full price) – 10% (discount) = 90% (discounted price)

This value is multiplied by the original price:

0.9 × £180 = £162

The result (£162) is the same whichever method you use. You can use the same methods to calculate the value of percentage increases. For example, if you had savings of £112.72 a year ago that you put in an account earning 4.3 per cent interest, you can calculate the current value of your savings.

Again there are two methods. Either calculate the actual amount by which your savings have increased:

4.3% of £112.72 = 4.3 ÷ 100 × £112.72 = £4.85

and add this to the original value of the savings:

£112.72 + £4.85 = £117.57

or calculate the percentage of your original savings you now have:

100% + 4.3% = 104.3%

and multiply this by the original value of your savings:

1.043 × £112.72 = £117.57

Again, these two methods produce the same result.

■ Conversions

It is helpful to be able to convert units within the metric system, and between the metric and the imperial system.

The metric system

Units of length – millimetres (mm), centimetres (cm), metres (m) and kilometres (km):

10 mm = 1 cm, 100 cm = 1 m, 1000 m = 1 km

Units of weight: grams (g), kilograms (kg) tonnes:

100 g = 1 kg, 1000 kg = 1 tonne.

The imperial system

Units of length: inches (in), feet (ft), yards (yds), miles.

12 inches = 1 foot, 3 feet = 1 yard (yd), 1760 yards = 1 mile

Units of weight: ounces (oz), pounds (lbs), stones, hundredweights (cwt), tons.

16 ounces = 1 pound, 14 pounds = 1 stone, 8 stone = 1 hundredweight, 1 ton = 20 cwt

Questions

1 The following diagram shows a structure that has been built as a support for a wooden shed. What is the value of the side a?

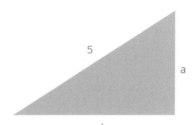

a 5;

b 4;

c 3;

d 2.

2 The mean weight of eight melons is 8 kg. The mean weight of two other melons is 10 kg. The mean weight of all 10 melons is:

a 8.4 kg;

b 9.0 kg;

c 9.6 kg;

d 10.0 kg.

3 In a survey of public transport, the time taken for a bus to complete a particular journey is recorded at various times of day throughout the week, and the mean and median times are calculated. One exceptionally long journey time caused by a road traffic accident could significantly affect the value of:

a the mean but not the median;

b the median but not the mean;

c both the mean and the median;

d neither the mean nor the median.

4 A survey has been carried out to find out how many televisions sixth-form students' families have in their homes. The results of the survey are displayed below.

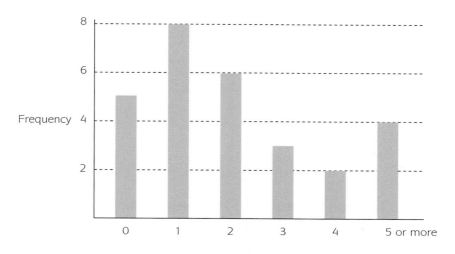

Number of television sets

How many of the following statistics can be calculated using the information displayed in the bar chart?

- The median.

- The range.

- The inter-quartile range.

a None of them.

b One of them.

c Two of them.

d All three of them.

5 From the information given in question 4, if a student is chosen at random from the class, what is the chance that there are more than three television sets in that student's family home?

a 3/14;

b 3/11;

c 9/28;

d 1/3.

6 Study the diagram below and identify which of the functions is an exponential function.

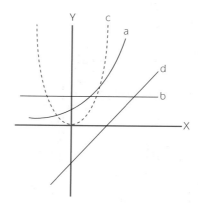

7 Given the function C = 100 + 1/2Y, which of the following is possible?

a When Y is 1000, C is 550.

b When Y is 800, C is 600.

c When Y is 700, C is 450.

d When Y is 600, C is 300.

8 A car's value depreciated at a rate of 12 per cent per year. When it was new it cost £9750. Its value, to the nearest £50, after three years was:

a £6250;

b £6650;

c £6900;

d £13 700.

9 If a students mark has increased by 25 per cent since last year, and this year her mark is 62.5 out of a hundred. What was her mark out of a hundred last year:

a 37.5;

b 47.5;

c 50.0;

d 52.5?

10 The ages in years of members of a primary school class are:

3, 3, 4, 5, 7, 7, 7, 8, 8, 8

Which one of the following is true:

a mean = median;

b mean > median > range;

c median > range > mean;

d median > mean > range.

11 A small catering firm makes the following charges for providing a meal:

For up to 50 people: £50 plus £3 per person.

For 51 to 100 people: £200 plus £2 per person in excess of 50.

The cost of a meal for 100 people is:

a £200;

b £250;

c £300;

d £350.

12 The table shows data about students in a class.

	Male	Female
Wears glasses	5	7
Does not wear glasses	11	6

What is the probability that a male student picked at random wears glasses:

a 5/29;

b 5/16;

c 5/12;

d 5/11?

13 It is necessary to convert a length in feet to its approximate equivalent in millimetres. Taking 2.5 cm to be 1 inch, you should multiply by which of the following:

a 1000/3;

b 300;

c 100/3;

d 1/300?

14 Two of the five playing cards that Colin has are aces. He shuffles the five cards, then puts them face down on the table. Madge takes a card and then takes another. The probability the she now has both of the aces is:

   a 1/10;

   b 4/25;

   c 1/5;

   d 2/5.

15 The number R, or reported cases per week of a particular illness over a period of two months, is to be modelled by the equation:

$$R = 50e^{1/5}$$

Which of the following graphs best illustrates how the number of reported cases will vary with time according to the model?

A   B   C   D

 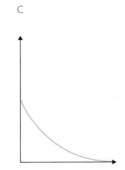 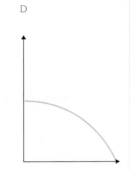

16 A gambler rolls two dice. What is the chance that he will throw a double:

   a 1 in 3;

   b 1 in 6;

   c 1 in 12;

   d 1 in 36?

Questions 17 to 19 relate to the following set of figures.

A basketball team records the following set of points scored over a 10-game series:

84 86 88 88 82 92 104 88 86 100

17 What is the range:

    a 16;

    b 4;

    c 20;

    d 22?

18 What is the mode:

    a 89.8;

    b 88;

    c 82;

    d 86?

19 What is the mean:

    a 82;

    b 88;

    c 89.8;

    d 88.5?

20 A variable is increasing in the following way: 2, 4, 16, 256. This is a good example of which of the following types of functions:

    a arithmetic;

    b inverse;

    c exponential;

    d many-one?

index

Page numbers in **bold** indicate where the term has been defined in the text